Nuclear Energy and Nuclear Proliferation

Other Titles in This Series

Westview Special Studies in International Relations

Nuclear Energy and Nuclear Proliferation: Japanese and American Views
Ryukichi Imai and Henry S. Rowen

Though the Carter administration came to office committed both to good U.S.-Japanese relations and to a more stringent nuclear nonproliferation policy, it soon became clear that these objectives were at cross-purposes, and that the dispute over nuclear nonproliferation policy threatened to shake the alliance between the two countries. Professors Imai and Rowen bring to light the major differences in the way Japanese and Americans perceive nuclear energy and nuclear proliferation. Their debate is not only an excellent discussion of the difficult nonproliferation issue, but also a highly instructive case study for those interested in U.S.-Japanese relations.

Ryukichi Imai is general manager, engineering, of the Japan Atomic Power Company and is also special assistant to Japan's minister of foreign affairs, dealing mainly with nuclear and arms control matters. Henry S. Rowen is professor of public management in the Graduate School of Business at Stanford University. He has served previously as president of the Rand Corporation, assistant director of the U.S. Bureau of the Budget, and deputy assistant secretary of defense for International Security Affairs.

Prepared under the auspices of the
Project on United States – Japan Relations
Stanford University

Nuclear Energy and Nuclear Proliferation: Japanese and American Views

Ryukichi Imai and Henry S. Rowen

Westview Press / Boulder, Colorado

Westview Special Studies in
International Relations

Copyright © 1980 by Westview Press, Inc.

Published in 1980 in the United States of America by
  Westview Press, Inc.
  5500 Central Avenue
  Boulder, Colorado 80301
  Frederick A. Praeger, Publisher

Library of Congress Cataloging in Publication Data
Imai, Ryukichi, 1929-
  Nuclear energy and nuclear proliferation.
  (Westview special studies in international relations)
  "Prepared under the auspices of the Project on United States–Japan Relations, Stanford University." 1. Nuclear nonproliferation. 2. United States—Foreign relations—Japan. 3. Japan—Foreign relations—United States. 4. Atomic energy—Japan. I. Rowen, Henry, joint author. II. Stanford University. Project on United States—Japan Relations. III. Title. IV. Series: Westview special studies in international relations.
  JX1974.73.I44   327'.174   79-16589
  ISBN 0-89158-667-9

Printed and bound in the United States of America

Contents

Appendixes

Foreword

The Carter administration came into office committed to good U.S.-Japan relations and also committed to a more stringent nuclear nonproliferation policy. In April 1977, these two objectives were visibly at cross-purposes, and the dispute over nuclear non-proliferation policy threatened to shake the alliance. The two authors of this book played useful behind-the-scenes roles in helping to moderate the shock waves. Their well-reasoned debate in these pages is not only an excellent discussion of the difficult non-proliferation issue but is also a highly instructive case study for those interested in the U.S.-Japan relationship.

The dilemma faced by the new administration in 1977 had deep roots and no easy solution. Since 1945, the dual aspects of nuclear energy had been recognized. U.S. efforts to deal with the dilemma had gone through various phases. After the failure in 1946 of the ambitious Baruch Plan for internationalizing nuclear energy, the United States tried to curb proliferation by restricting access to technology. In 1953, Eisenhower's Atoms for Peace proposal shifted the approach to one of promoting technology transfer in return for development of an international regime of safeguards and inspection. The international safeguards system established under the International Atomic Energy Agency (IAEA) in 1957 and reinforced by the Nonproliferation Treaty in 1968 seemed to have solved the proliferation problem in the early 1970s.

Complacency was shaken, however, by the 1974 Indian detonation of a nuclear device using technology and materials obtained from Canada and the United States for peaceful purposes. Alarm was further increased, particularly in the Canadian Parliament and the United States Congress, by proposed U.S. reactor sales to Egypt and Israel, and by French and German plans to go beyond reactor sales by providing reprocessing plants that could extract weapons-usable plutonium from spent reactor fuels in Korea, Pakistan, and Brazil. This period of anxiety and turmoil, which began in 1974, helps explain many provisions of the U.S. Nonproliferation Act of 1978, which Imai criticizes in his essay.

In the eyes of the new Carter administration officials, events in the international nuclear energy arena were like bicycles speeding downhill without brakes and approaching a sharp curve as plutonium fuels replaced the familiar (less readily weapons-usable) low enriched uranium fuels. The policy objective was to put brakes on the bicycles—to buy time to strengthen institutions and technology before accidents occurred at the curve. It was recognized that technology would spread with time, but that policy could affect the rate and conditions of spread so as to be better able to cope with potentially destabilizing effects. The wide spread of facilities involving weapons-usable materials—in 1974 the IAEA projected some forty-six countries using plutonium by 1990—before institutional and technical improvements were in place would almost certainly have ruptured the international safeguards regime that had been so laboriously constructed over the past two decades. Although the nuclear fuel cycle is not the only path to a weapons capability, there was evidence that some countries intended to misuse allegedly peaceful facilities. Thus, in April 1977, President Carter announced policy changes toward the use of plutonium in the United States and called for an International Nuclear Fuel Cycle Evaluation to develop more realistic estimates of the timing, risks, and institutional opportunities for various aspects of the peaceful uses of nuclear energy.

For Japan, the world's third largest economic power and almost totally dependent upon imported energy, insecurity of energy supply loomed much larger than any military insecurity related to proliferation. For the Japanese, the salient event of 1974 was not the Indian explosion, but the aftermath of the Arab oil embargo. In the eyes of Japanese officials, the relevant bicycle metaphor would be a cyclist crossing a desert with only a small canteen of water and no time to lose before reaching the other side. The fact that neither nuclear energy nor, more specifically, the use of plutonium fuels in existing reactors would significantly reduce Japanese dependence on imported oil during this century simply reinforced Japanese officials' belief in the need for haste. They feared that any questions, pauses, or alterations of the fuel cycle plans that had been established in an earlier period might fracture the fragile social consensus underlying nuclear energy. Moreover, until recently, Americans in and out of government had advocated the early use of plutonium, and the officials of the new administration who stressed nonproliferation were strangers to the familiar transnational network of the nuclear energy world.

Thus, when President Carter announced that the United States was going to defer reprocessing and the use of plutonium in existing reactors and was going to restructure its breeder reactor research and development program to stress safer fuel cycles rather than early commercialization, there was considerable consternation in Japan. To make matters worse, Japan was just in the final stages of completing its first pilot scale reprocessing plant at Tokai Mura, and the existing agreement for nuclear cooperation between the United States and Japan provided for U.S. approval rights over any Japanese reprocessing of fuel that had originally come from the United States. Thus, at the same time that President Carter was deferring the reprocessing of U.S. fuel at home (over the strong opposition of U.S. industry and congressional critics), he was being asked to make an exception to permit the Japanese to do what U.S. industry was not allowed to do at home. The domestic politics of the issue became heated in both countries. Eventually, and with informal contributions from Ryukichi Imai and Henry Rowen, a compromise was reached. That compromise is reproduced here in the Appendix.

The Tokai crisis served to intensify a broad range of consultations between Japanese and Americans on nuclear issues. One effect has been the beginning of a convergence of perspectives as Americans become more sensitive to Japanese energy security concerns and as Japanese begin to perceive their other security interests involved in the proliferation dimensions of nuclear energy. Fortunately, Japan's own intentions were never an issue, and the alliance partners shared an interest, albeit unequally weighted, in both the energy security and military security aspects of the nuclear proliferation problem. Compromise was possible. That important differences still remain, however, will be readily apparent in the following essays.

Aside from the substance of the nuclear issue, what lessons can we learn about U.S.-Japan relations from this case? I see at least five.

First, the U.S.-Japan alliance reflects deep interests in both countries. Because the alliance is rooted in reality, it has resilience. Although shocks occur, there is also an awareness of the importance of the relationship that helps contain the effects.

Second, tensions are certain to exist in the alliance because the military and economic resource situations of the two countries are so different. It is inevitable that their positions and perceptions would often differ—witness the relative weighing of the two dimensions of security in the essays of these two highly sophisticated authors—even if there were no linguistic and cultural differences.

Third, both governments need to think carefully about the meaning of leadership in a world where U.S. dominance has diminished. Three common measures of leadership—to command, to go first, to induce—correspond to hegemony, unilateralism, and multilateralism. It is no longer possible for the United States to command, yet multilateralism often means immobilism. Imai correctly warns against too much unilateralism; yet in today's world, the United States must often rely upon a combination of unilateralism and multilateral inducement if collective paralysis is to be avoided in complex transnational issues with deep roots in domestic politics. The Carter decision to defer reprocessing was necessary to avert the international collapse that would almost certainly have followed safeguards violations had "business as usual" continued in the nuclear area. In the words of *The Economist,* "Thanks to the timely stubbornness of President Carter among others, [proliferation] is not at present seen to be increasing as fast as might be expected in a world whose reactors are creating plutonium at an ever-growing rate in an ever-growing number of countries."*

Whatever the merits in this nuclear case, leadership in the current period may often involve decisions like Carter's. If this is true,

---

*The Economist (London), November 11, 1978, p. 16

then it behooves both governments to pay more attention to early warnings. Certainly the signs of congressional intent to take unilateral action on the nuclear energy issue were visible more than a year in advance. Yet, when I visited Tokyo in September 1976, I found few officials responsive to my suggestions that the nuclear issue was likely to become a major item on the U.S.-Japan agenda.

A fourth lesson follows from the third. In the past, Japan has tended to seek special exceptions to universal rules. Less attention is paid to the burden of leadership in setting and maintaining rules that are required if stable international regimes are to govern global issues. In their essays below, Imai and Rowen discuss the dangers of general formulations in the nuclear issue; yet they are also aware of the problems that discriminatory solutions in the U.S.-Japan context create with other countries. In addition to seeking exceptions, Japanese national interest will increasingly have to be defined in terms of sharing the problems involved in the assumption of leadership in establishing and maintaining international regimes.

Finally, both countries need to pay more attention to the manner in which they conduct their dialogues. Large delegations, formal parleys, and summit meetings probably produced more misunderstanding than real communication in the nuclear case discussed here. Some of the most fruitful communications were the small and informal ones, such as those in which Imai and Rowen participated, and at which the basic issues could be discussed. Many more such dialogues are going to be necessary if the two countries are to develop early warning systems and coordinate their policies with a minimum of shocks. This book is a useful step in that direction.

Joseph S. Nye
Cambridge, Massachusetts

Preface

This book is a product of discussions and research organized by Stanford University's Project on U.S.-Japan Relations. This project was initiated in 1974 to stimulate research and training that would systematically bring academic expertise to bear on the task of creating a better understanding of problems affecting relations between the United States and Japan. As a component of Stanford's Arms Control and Disarmament Program, the project has placed major emphasis on problems of international security and arms control in Asia.

One of the chief goals of the project is the fostering of a Japanese-American dialogue aimed at identifying areas in which divergent perceptions may lead to misunderstanding between the two countries. Policy-related questions are analyzed, through international meetings and joint research, with a long-term perspective and a particular emphasis on exploring the basic assumptions underlying Japanese and U.S. views. Where appropriate, efforts are made to develop specific policy recommendations consistent with each country's interests. The present pair of studies by Ryukichi Imai and Henry S. Rowen brings to light major differences in the way Japanese and Americans perceive problems related to nuclear energy and nuclear proliferation. To help clarify their differences, each author has written a commentary on his counterpart's position.

The two authors bring impressive credentials to this endeavor. Imai is general manager, Engineering, of the Japan Atomic Power Company. He is also a special assistant to the minister of foreign affairs, dealing mainly with nuclear and arms control matters. He

Preface

holds a doctorate in nuclear engineering from the University of Tokyo, as well as master's degrees in East Asian studies from Harvard and in international relations from the Fletcher School of Law and Diplomacy. Rowen is professor of public management in the Graduate School of Business at Stanford University. Trained in engineering and economics at the Massachusetts Institute of Technology and at Oxford, Rowen has served as president of the Rand Corporation, assistant director of the Bureau of the Budget, and deputy assistant secretary of defense for international security affairs. He is a recognized expert on nuclear energy problems and chairs the International Energy Group at Stanford.

By pinpointing and explaining differences between Japanese and U.S. perspectives, this book makes an important contribution to the process of building a foundation for better understanding between the two countries. In addition, the two authors' involvement in this study gave them an unusual opportunity to make a more direct contribution to that process. Rowen and Imai became a useful unofficial channel for frank discussion of the controversial issues relating to the Carter administration's new nonproliferation policy and Japan's plan to open a plutonium separation facility at Tokai Mura. In the course of their several meetings in Tokyo and Washington during the spring of 1977, Imai and Rowen were able to clarify the issues and to formulate elements of a strategy for their resolution. Since Imai was directly involved in the government-to-government negotiations and Rowen was in contact with key officials in Washington, the results of their in-depth discussions were fed directly into the policymaking process. The contributions of Imai and Rowen are noted in this book's foreword, written by Joseph S. Nye. Mr. Nye, professor of government at Harvard University, served from 1977 to 1979 as deputy to the under secretary of state for security assistance, science, and technology. He also chaired the National Security Council Group on Nonproliferation that formulated the Carter administration's policy.

The present studies were undertaken as a follow-up to a conference held at Stanford on April 29-30, 1976. That meeting was convened to provide an opportunity for Imai and several other Japanese specialists to exchange views with a number of U.S. experts in the nuclear energy field. Participants (with their then-current affiliations) in that meeting, besides Imai and Rowen, included the following: John Barton, Stanford; Harold Bengelsdorf, Department of State; Thomas Connolly, Stanford; Victor Gilinsky, Nuclear Regulatory Commission; John Gray, International Energy Associates; Joseph Harned, Atlantic Council; Gerard Helfrich, Energy Research and Development Agency; Spurgeon Keeny, Mitre Corporation; Paul Langer, Rand Corporation; Makoto Momoi, National Defense College of Japan; Koichiro Obata, Foreign Ministry of Japan; Ashton O'Donnell, Bechtel; Herbert Scoville, Arms Control Association; Rudolph Sher, Stanford; Chauncey Starr, Electric Power Research Institute; Toshide Takeshita, Institute for Policy Science, Tokyo; Vince Taylor, Pan-Heuristics; Charles Van Doren, Arms Control and Disarmament Agency; Lawrence Weiler, Stanford; and Herbert York, University of California, San Diego. For additional discussion of the results of this conference and other meetings on related subjects, the reader should consult Franklin B. Weinstein (ed.), *U.S.-Japan Relations and the Security of East Asia: The Next Decade* (Westview Press, 1978).

Professor Rowen's contribution is an adaptaton of a report "Toward A New Consensus on Nuclear Technology" prepared under contract with Pan-Heuristics for the Arms Control and Disarmament Agency. The judgments in the original report and in this adaptation are those of the author and do not necessarily reflect the veiws of ACDA or any other agency of the U.S. government.

Financial support for the 1976 conference and follow-up studies was provided by the Sumitomo Fund for Policy Research Studies (administered by the Japan Society) and the State Department's Office of External Research. Professor Rowen's March 1977 visit to Japan was made possible by the National Defense College of Japan. The initial drafts were revised and expanded for discussion at a general meeting of the project held in Hakone, Japan, on July 2-5, 1978. Further revisions were undertaken following that meeting. The Japan Center for International Exchange helped in many ways to facilitate this collaborative effort. Of course, none of

the agencies mentioned above bear any responsibility for the con-
tents of these studies. The index was prepared by Betsy Ingram.

Franklin B. Weinstein
Director
Project on U.S.-Japan Relations
Stanford, California

Part 1
A Japanese View

Ryukichi Imai

Introduction to Part 1

For many years, nuclear nonproliferation has been a matter of concern primarily to the United States. Other countries have accommodated to nonproliferation's constraints because the United States insisted on it so passionately. Today, however, many of those countries are questioning how much longer they can comply with the requirements set by the United States. At the same time, it is evident that they will continue to support nonproliferation as a matter of principle.

Historically, nonproliferation has been the narrow concern of a band of experts whose basic inclination is more technical and procedural than political or social. Since World War II, many ideas essentially technical or procedural in content have been advanced to prevent nuclear proliferation, but the results have not been altogether satisfactory. Technically feasible proposals are often politically unworkable or legally imprecise, whereas politically acceptable solutions often lack technical or logical rigor. Because of the frequency with which U.S. nonproliferation policy has been reversed and the confusion that has accompanied Washington's fuel-supply policies, it is doubtful that still another set of U.S. proposals can find much credibility among other nations.

The basic tenets of nuclear nonproliferation are simple enough—so simple that from time to time newcomers think they have come upon important new truths and begin proposing new policy provisions. In fact, practically all the logically conceivable solutions have been examined at one time or another during the brief but complex history of nuclear power. "New truths," when pressed enthusiastically, tend to annoy the specialists, who know from experience that the technology and the associated considerations involved are not so simple in either their social or their industrial implications.

Instead of additional proposals for procedural repairs, what is needed today is a comprehensive new analysis of the problem against a wider background—an analysis that considers not only the time-honored ways of thinking of the United States but also the different perceptions of threat and national security held by other countries. It is important to realize that nuclear power has come to symbolize a general social philosophy about the role of technology in modern society, a philosophy that extends well beyond matters of energy and defense. As evidenced by the concern now given to problems of environmental pollution and nuclear safety, modern large-scale technology has introduced completely new types and dimensions of "threats" to man's social and biological environment. In almost all areas of human activity, technology poses threats, but the risks are more often long-term possibilities than immediate certainties. Where a technology yields obviously adverse side effects, restrictive measures are of course needed; but the relentless urging of unrealistic or absolutist hypotheses can in time lead to the denial of all practical benefits of the technology—even though it was in order to produce those benefits that the technology came to be widely employed.

The U.S. view of nuclear nonproliferation is a product of that country's own unique history, and it is immaterial whether the U.S. approach is right or wrong. The U.S. experience in the field of military uses of nuclear energy has been unlike that of any other nation, and it is natural that U.S. experience should dominate its thinking about nuclear topics generally. But people outside the United States have often failed to appreciate the uniqueness of the U.S. experience—or, for that matter, to explain to the Americans that other countries may therefore view nuclear technology in quite a different light. Nor has the United States bent much effort to explain to others the real source of its concern; nations that have not had the U.S. militiary experience thus find it difficult to comprehend why nuclear nonproliferation should be an issue of such overriding importance. The lack of continuity in U.S. policy from one administration to the next has exacerbated this problem. Such international dialogue as has occurred has been limited mainly to the experts and to points of procedure.

As a first step toward understanding the nonproliferation problem, it is essential that we consider the issue in its broader social and political context, giving due regard to the implications of different national experiences. In many quarters, there is growing concern that the political leadership of the world—and especially of the United States because of its great weight in this issue—come to see the problem in this light, so that the formulation of future nuclear nonproliferation policy may rest on a sounder basis.

1
The Confused History
of Nuclear Nonproliferation

In the early postwar years, the principal manifestation of U.S. concern about limiting the global spread of nuclear weapons was the Acheson-Lilienthal Plan of 1946, which became the basis of the Baruch Plan presented to the United Nations in the same year. During this period the Soviet Union obviously gave the United States the most concern in this respect. The technology of nuclear weapons was so sophisticated and so closely guarded that no other country was considered likely to seek it, especially in light of the heavy burden of postwar reconstruction. The Americans refused to share the technology even with the British, their wartime allies (and at the time potentially a predecessor in the actual exploitation of the technology), because of the fear that the information might become available to the Russians—either through Soviet occupation of England or through what the United States regarded as rather loose control of secrecy in the United Kingdom. The possibility that West Germany or Japan might try to acquire the technology was considered remote but not disregarded entirely. Under the circumstances, it was inevitable that the USSR would refuse to support the U.S. scheme for the international control of nuclear technology.

U.S. Custodianship by Self-Appointment

Even as early as the Acheson-Lilienthal Plan, the U.S. posture was unmistakably that of God-appointed guardian of this dangerous technology. President Truman said as much in his public statements, and Lilienthal's feelings on the subject were expressed in many entries in his private journal. Adopting this posture was natural enough, for no one else was in possession of certain critical information or in a position to convert abstract theories of nuclear physics into the reality of nuclear weapons through the investment of enormous amounts of time, money, and expertise. The Manhattan Project became the prototype for the organization of *Big Science*, which has seemed to dominate the world ever since. Very few people, however, were astute enough and farsighted enough to perceive the growing role of science and technology as a force that could both promote and threaten the fundamental well-being of humanity. And very few, if any, could comprehend fully the ways in which the rapidly expanding arsenal of nuclear weapons had basically changed the concept of war.

The custodianship posture grew firm in American minds and came to have a dominating influence on the formulation of U.S. nonproliferation policy. The custodianship role was never fully acknowledged by the rest of the world, however. The most obvious dissenters were the Soviet Union, China, and France. But others, though they may have had neither the desire nor the ability to penetrate the secrets of nuclear weapons, had serious reservations about the U.S. position. Today, U.S. leaders talk about the loss of a dominance that had once allowed Washington to dictate nuclear policy to the world. The observation is accurate. But even when the United States was in a position to dictate policy to the Free World, it never had won the hearts of its allies.

The Period of Proliferation

When the first Russian atomic bomb was exploded in 1949, the initial, very clearly defined goal of U.S. nonproliferation policy was defeated. What ensued was an accelerating escalation of the quality and quantity of nuclear weapons in both camps, including the most powerful and most versatile warheads. We need not go over that ground here, but it is clear that neither nonproliferation nor arms control was a central consideration during the first years of the 1950s.

Many factors, then, explain the onset of the Atoms for Peace policy at the end of 1953. It might be argued that if nonproliferation had been more important to the United States than the maintenance of a strong nuclear industry or outmaneuvering the

Russians on every front, it would not have promoted with such enthusiasm the spread of nuclear power for peaceful purposes. But it is true, nonetheless, that all bilateral agreements entered into by the United States during this period contained provisions granting the United States power to dictate the disposition of plutonium and to ensure the maintenance of safeguards. Responsibility for the safeguards was to be transferred to the International Atomic Energy Agency as soon as it was ready to take on that burden.

It is important to remember that information about such matters as uranium enrichment and plutonium production, now public knowledge, was then available only to a handful of people in the United States and the Soviet Union. As far as the rest of the world was concerned, virtually all nuclear information was locked in a tightly guarded black box; and it was only in 1955, at the Geneva Conference, that the United States released any of it — and even then no more than some information concerning reactors. The recipients of this information were more than happy to comply with the safeguards and other nonproliferation measures required by the United States in exchange for such exciting new information — partly because many of them did not see nonproliferation as a serious matter.

Two other developments of the period are worth noting. One is the emergence of a new cadre of atoms-for-peace bureaucrats, people whose technical backgrounds were for the most part at substantial variance with those of the weapons people in the U.S. Atomic Energy Commission (AEC). These bureaucrats rapidly developed their own empire, and it is they who have been entrusted with the important task of administering the U.S. nonproliferation policy, in both its domestic and international aspects.

The second development concerns the psychological distinction between military and peaceful uses of nuclear energy. The Atoms for Peace plan, as spelled out in the 1954 Atomic Energy Act, opened up relevant portions of the U.S. monopoly on nuclear power-producing reactors, while preserving the U.S. monopoly in matters relating to weapons production and submarine propulsion. Except for some important details of hardware production, however, it is often difficult to distinguish between military and nonmilitary technology. In fact, some people have argued that the United States did not really object to the partial erosion of its monopoly in the military field, and they point to the later discussions concerning the proposed multilateral force (MLF) as evidence.

The Nth Country Problem and the Nonproliferation Treaty

The "nth country problem" did not become a subject for serious discussion until the early 1960s, owing partly to the prevailing psychology of the 1950s. Three other factors that remained valid well into the 1960s need to be considered.

First, although the Atoms for Peace plan instantly stimulated worldwide interest in the potential role of nuclear energy in power generation, it was clearly a plan that would bear fruit only in the distant future; nuclear energy could not meet the immediate needs of postwar reconstruction and development. The technology was still very much in the developmental stage, and it was only in the middle 1960s that nuclear power reactors of appreciable size began to deliver electricity to the power grid. Moreover, the uranium-enrichment and plutonium-extraction technologies were available only to the nuclear weapons states; not even the most advanced of the other industrialized nations had access to these technologies. It was not until the close of the 1960s that countries like West Germany and Japan announced ambitious nuclear power programs, and it was only after the oil crisis of 1973 that the rest of the world joined in the march of nuclear power generation. Only then did the enrichment and reprocessing technologies begin to show serious signs of proliferating beyond the circle of nuclear-weapons states.

Second, the safeguards drafted by the International Atomic Energy Agency provided at least psychological reassurance against proliferation, even though the technology for implementing safeguards was not actually realized until the 1970s. Though the provision for safeguards was written into the IAEA statute in 1957, it was only in 1961 that the first implementation document was prepared for reactors of up to 100 Megawatts (MW) thermal output, hardly a commercial nuclear power station. It was in 1971 that the agency finally worked out a comprehensive document of technically satisfactory safeguard procedures covering all phases of the nuclear fuel cycle. Even in that final document, however, the safeguarding provisions for enrichment and reprocessing plants remained incomplete. This situation reflected simply the fact that large-scale enrichment and reprocessing facilities did not yet exist in the portion of the world's nuclear industry that was subject to safeguards—the procedures had not yet been worked out because there was no real need.

At the same time, many observers, failing to examine the real nature of IAEA safeguards, found it convenient to believe that the safeguards would prevent nuclear proliferation across national boundaries. In reality, the safeguards could not prevent the proliferation of weapons potential; they could only prevent the diversion of the potential into actual weapons production. Preventing the proliferation of important technologies is a political and, very often, economic problem, not a technical one; and technical devices such as safeguards cannot possibly solve what is basically a political and economic problem. A handful of people, myself included, have labored to make this point understood, but it seems evident that clarifying the limitations of safeguards runs counter to the vested interests of the world's nuclear bureaucracies. The Nonproliferation Treaty (NPT), which provides for freedom to carry on research and development and for the dissemination of information, clearly was meant to prevent the proliferation of weapons and other nuclear explosive devices but not the spread of the attendant technology. The IAEA safeguards, which are the major instrument of the NPT, were regarded as a powerful means of linking these two distinct concerns; not until the Salzburg Conference of 1977 did it become generally known that safeguards alone may in fact not be particularly powerful.

Third, not since the People's Republic of China conducted its first nuclear test in 1964 has any industrial country seemed to be seriously contemplating the acquisition of nuclear weapons. In particular, West Germany and Japan, the two nations considered most capable of undertaking a nuclear weapons program, have shown no such interest, except for occasional domestic debates about the desirability of "retaining the nuclear option." Their official disavowals have been made the more convincing by an objective assessment of the costs and benefits of undertaking nuclear-armament programs: for these countries, the production of nuclear armaments on any meaningful scale would entail prohibitive risk and cost, in both political and economic terms, and highly dubious returns. The role of the NPT in this dialectic was to confirm publicly the superpowers' agreement to avoid nuclear war and to declare that other technologically advanced countries would not seek to change the global status quo through the acquisition of nuclear explosive capabilities.

Thus, it might be argued that the nth country problem or the so-called n + 1 country problem was primarily an interesting exercise with little relation to reality. Proliferation was not then at the head of the political agenda, and, so it was thought, whatever problems existed could be adequately handled through the development of IAEA safeguards.

The Changing World of Energy

By the late 1960s, the U.S. Atomic Energy Commission and the nuclear agencies abroad had begun to prepare for a new era of industrial nuclear power. It was becoming increasingly clear that among the many different reactor concepts that had been considered in the earlier period, the light-water reactors of U.S. design alone would play a predominant role for the rest of the century. Commercial competition began to develop among the leading industrial countries. In 1970, however, the U.S. Atomic Energy Commission declared that the United States would not be able to keep feeding the world's light-water reactors with uranium enriched in U.S. facilities. After some complicated negotiations, the AEC announced that continued U.S. enrichment services would be made conditional on the willingness of purchasers to recycle plutonium in their reactors, thus reducing the burden on U.S. enrichment plants. Thereafter, throughout the world, efforts were increased to develop both independent enrichment capabilities and plutonium-extraction facilities. An apparent shortage of uranium to feed all of the light-water reactors then planned added to the urgency of developing the plutonium-recycling technology. During the early 1970s, the rest of the world watched with considerable concern the developing debates between Republicans and Democrats over who—public or private enterprise—should take over the enrichment business in the United States, and the debates between the AEC and the Arms Control and Disarmament

Agency (ACDA) over whether to encourage or discourage nuclear export. None of the compromise solutions, such as a government enrichment corporation or multilateral reprocessing centers, seemed very realistic. (It might be added that the world business community was not impressed by the rather glib bureaucratic proposals of the time. As one who participated in the evaluation of many of these U.S.-originated concepts, I can attest to the cool response of at least the Japanese business community.)

The 1973 oil crisis and the 1974 Indian nuclear detonation had dramatic impacts. The uncertain future of oil supplies and prices made the nuclear alternative suddenly more attractive. The Indian test demonstrated that a nation could develop a nuclear explosive device solely on the basis of Atoms for Peace technology. Growing nationalism among the resource-rich less developed countries and a widening gap between the nations of the North and the South suggested an increasing trend toward confrontation, with an increasing number of Third World countries ready and able to challenge the existing international economic order, possibly with nuclear explosives. The nuclear proliferation problem thus began to take on a new dimension, which was immediately seized upon by U.S. politicians and intellectuals recently freed from preoccupation with the protracted and embarrassing experiences of Vietnam and Watergate. Two simultaneous developments defined this new dimension: (1) nuclear power had developed to the point where it was now expected to serve the growing energy needs of the world, and this was seen as requiring not only reactors but development of the entire fuel cycle; and (2) nonaligned Third World countries had acquired the political clout to challenge the world order dictated by the nuclear superpowers.

What most observers found especially troublesome was the multifaceted threat that the nuclear-proliferated world of the future seemed to pose. The central issues now concerned such matters as the French sale of reprocessing technology to South Korea and Pakistan, West Germany's sale of the same technology to Brazil, and U.S. exports of special nuclear material to India. These developments seemed to be alarming indications that some less-developed countries were contemplating the acquisition of nuclear technologies that could hardly be justified on economic or industrial grounds.

Unfortunately, within the executive and legislative branches of the U.S. government, the responsibility for taking steps to deal with this new situation fell to the same old nuclear bureaucracy, with its predisposition to work from a narrow technical background and to handle the nonproliferation problem primarily through procedural arrangements. Although the nonproliferation issue may have looked the same as before, the changing international scene had in fact given the problem a completely new dimension. For the United States, an appropriate response would have been a thorough reevaluation of overall global strategy with respect to energy, trade, defense, natural resources, and, more generally, the whole issue of global interdependence. Any meaningful solution of the nuclear proliferation problem should also have begun with a careful consideration of present and future alliances. But the Carter administration's initial approach to the problem was simply to ignore history and to propose a grossly simplified technical and procedural solution without regard for the political intricacies involved.

At the same time, there has been a major shift in the way the economic feasibility of nuclear power is evaluated. At the initial Atoms for Peace stage, it was anticipated that nuclear power would eventually be able to compete favorably with conventional power generation as the nuclear industry began to develop economies of scale. By the middle 1970s, however, the economic picture had grown quite confused: more stringent regulatory requirements for safety and for environmental protection had increased the capital costs of nuclear power stations; growing public opposition to the installation of nuclear facilities had dramatically lengthened the time needed to construct those facilities; and uncertainties relating to the supply of uranium, the cost of enrichment, the handling of spent fuel, and the final disposition of nuclear waste all helped to make nuclear power look very expensive. No one can now state with authority whether nuclear power will prove to be cheaper than oil- or coal-fired power stations or other sources of energy, because in no case have the environmental and other costs been clearly defined. The only certainty is that energy, whatever the source, will be expensive.

Some observers blame this situation on decisions to concentrate on the development of nuclear power at the expense of alternative technologies. Though that may be, nuclear power has reached a level of industrial maturity unattained by any of the other new energy sources. Although public support for the development of nuclear power has generally waned over the years, that decline is related, at least in part, to the general economic well-being of society— many of the more immediate threats are being dealt with and are thus making way for a concentration on the more indirect and remote threats. And many of the "threats" that have contributed to nuclear power's decline in popularity tend to be based on considerations that are more philosophical than real. The widespread concern about nuclear safety, about the hijacking of nuclear weapons, and about nuclear proliferation is based not on past experience but on hypotheses of what might happen. There are, however, limits beyond which only the very prosperous can afford to pursue means for dealing with the possibility that various terrifying scenarios might someday be acted out. The social, economic, and political costs attending such efforts are likely to be staggering.

Sitting comfortably amid its natural resources, the United States is inclined to pursue these threat scenarios farther than any other country can afford to; moreover, the Americans' immediate experience in the development and handling of nuclear weapons encourages them to proceed on such a path. However sincere its intentions may be, the United States is inevitably a slave to its own peculiar mode of thinking. A general failure to appreciate this pattern leads many to see in the current U.S. nonproliferation policy a hidden motivation, an indulgence of self-interest in seeking commercial advantage in the international nuclear energy market. How unfortunate, then, that those responsible for U.S. policy are often newcomers, unfamiliar with U.S. history and with the patterns and conflicts in nuclear policies abroad.

2

Areas of Conflict

Before examining the kinds of nuclear proliferation that should be prevented and some possible ways of preventing them, we shall do well to consider the context of the problem—energy alternatives, the current state of nuclear power, the international fuel-cycle market, the problem of technology transfer, changing views on the role of Big Science, and the implications of the political atmosphere of détente. Each of these is, in some measure, an area of potential conflict.

Energy Alternatives

Although energy has become a central concern in both domestic and international affairs, in many countries coordination between long-standing domestic energy policy and the new international realities is poor indeed. Take, for example, pricing policies. The current debate in the United States over deregulation and crude-oil equalization, or the OPEC debate over long-range, real-term pricing with the declining value of the dollar reflects such diverse considerations as consumer protection, resource conservation and development, energy dependence, divestiture, world inflation and the imbalance in the world's monetary institutions, and OPEC production levels. It is obvious that those diverse domestic and international considerations are not at all well organized into a comprehensive policy package.

Postwar economic prosperity has owed much to the availability of cheap oil and gas, and the industrially advanced countries have ensured their availability through global control of both production and prices. Since that control has been lost and the consumption of oil has risen to about 20 billion barrels a year—a level in excess of the average annual discovery rate—the need for a fundamental change in energy-consumption patterns has become apparent. Furthermore, anticipated limits on production capacity in the Arabian peninsula suggest that during the 1980s the world will no longer be able to support a 3 percent annual increase in energy consumption. Given the distribution of available OPEC oil, the countries of the South will be at an advantage vis-à-vis those of the North. Thus, there are strong incentives for the industrial nations of the North to develop alternative sources of energy, not only for the next century but even for the next ten to fifteen years. Although there is a good deal of talk about non-OPEC hydrocarbon resources, these are not proved reserves. *Policy options* in the face of enormous uncertainties in the balance of supply and demand seem to be the central concern of many governments.

Except for countries with abundant conventional resources of their own, the continued maintenance of energy security will depend on how soon the new energy technologies can be made to achieve industrial feasibility and penetrate the market. These considerations put nuclear fusion and the large-scale application of solar energy into the realm of possibility for the middle of the twenty-first century. The fast breeder reactor, coal gasification, and synthetic oil are possibilities by the year 2000. The only meaningful options for the near term are the employment of light-water reactors on a large scale and the more economic use of coal. Although the role of nuclear power in the world energy situation is somewhat uncertain today—it will not achieve by the mid-1980s the 15 million barrels-per-day oil equivalent that some had expected back in 1973—this does not negate the importance of nuclear power as an energy option.

Energy conservation is also important, to be sure, but its potential value is massively greater in the United States than elsewhere: more than half of U.S. energy consumption lies in transportation and in commercial and household uses, and U.S. per capita energy consumption is seven times the world average (ten times the world average excluding the United States) and roughly three to four times the per capita consumption of countries like West Germany, France, and Japan.

Because of the enormous cost of developing and deploying new energy technologies, it is obviously preferable that the technologies adopted for the next ten to fifteen years be capable of extension into the longer term. Thus, if coal is adopted for immediate use in thermal power stations, efforts should also be made to develop better pollution controls, more economic transportation systems, and gasification or liquefaction techniques that would make possible the use of coal on a very large scale. Similarly, if the nuclear route is chosen, the approach should be linked firmly to the development of the plutonium-burning technology, rather than to a mindless burning of the limited uranium resources available. (The debate whether the uranium supply will last until 1995 or until 2010 is meaningless in any responsible plan.) Nor do many countries enjoy such an abundance of resources and high technology that they may luxuriate in an additional two or three years of study before settling on an optimum strategy. Most nations must act immediately: a loss of momentum in the development of technology would be fatal. This point will be even clearer if we remember that to construct and operate light-water reactor nuclear power plants, or any of the other fuel-cycle facilities using known technology, requires more than ten years' lead time, and bringing a new energy technology to industrial production levels requires more than a quarter-century.

The Current State of Nuclear Power

Again, as against the expectations of the early years of Atoms for Peace, the economic attractiveness of nuclear power is declining. Society's view of nuclear power has also undergone a major change. Nuclear power has come to be regarded by many as a major safety risk, even though (1) the release of radioactivity from a nuclear power plant during normal operation is limited to one-twentieth of the natural radioactivity at the site boundary, (2) the probability of a reactor accident that would kill 100 people is calculated at less than one case in a million years, and (3) the total radiation from all of the light-water reactor activities anticipated in the United States up to the year 2000 would be about 1 percent of what is in the normal environment. To be sure, as they have accumulated experience, engineers have found that the technical problems of handling the intense radiation created by nuclear fission are much more severe than they had originally anticipated. And problems related to the "back end" of the fuel cycle (the spent fuel) and to concerns about proliferation have compounded these difficulties. Today, no one is especially sanguine about the prospects for expanding the range of nuclear energy uses beyond the generation of electricity; and no one any longer states with conviction that nuclear power can with certainty meet the energy needs of the future if only enough money, effort, and resources are committed to its development. The fact is, however, that among *all* the energy technologies pessimism is endemic. "Growth and progress" have given way, in the world's thinking, to "limits to growth" — and not just in the field of nuclear energy.

The reasons why countries choose to develop nuclear power may be many. Nuclear power is of course merely an option whose contribution to the total world energy picture may not exceed 10 percent in the coming ten to twenty years. Some countries are counting on greater-than-average contributions from nuclear power in the full knowledge that success is not assured, but given their energy needs and the lack of promising alternatives, they simply cannot afford to forgo its promise.

In some countries, current levels of technological and industrial development may argue for the exploitation of other resources to meet energy needs. It has also been argued that import-substitution industries are a poor initial choice for the less-developed countries. But nuclear power, as a symbol of technological advancement, is a source of prestige both domestically and internationally, and for many governments this may be a very important political consideration. Some countries may plan assiduously for ways to move from nuclear power generation to the manufacture of nuclear weapons, but that is extremely unlikely. Even those who might harbor such thoughts for the distant future would not have enough detailed knowledge to calculate the actual distance that a country lacking an adequate technical and social infrastructure would have to travel in order to achieve such ends. It is also a well accepted thesis that, given a choice, a country with nuclear weapons interests will not select the power reactor route, which is the least cost-effective path to nuclear explosives.

If the experience of Japan's industrialization a century ago is any indication, the consequences of any particular industrialization process will be secondary, compared to the importance of industrialization itself. Although logic may lead outsiders to conclude that the acquisition of plutonium technology will lead inevitably to an orientation toward nuclear weapons (and this may well turn out to be the reality), one can scarcely insist that the country seeking the technology does not genuinely believe plutonium to be an integral part of the nuclear technology they require now. For that reason alone, it is important that the world community be tendered a convincing and thoroughgoing explanation of the true nature of plutonium technology and of the fact that only nations or consortia with a mature, large-scale nuclear industry will be able to afford its pursuit. It may be useful to add that arguments against plutonium-burning reactors on the basis of cost are patently unconvincing, particularly coming from those who were preaching the reverse just several years ago.

The International Fuel-Cycle Market

In several respects, the nuclear fuel-cycle industry is uniquely international. Uranium reserves are found in only a few areas of the world. Excluding the United States, there is no region in which anticipated future demand is matched by potential supply. By definition, then, uranium is an international commodity. Moreover, newly discovered reserves tend to be relatively inaccessible, for geographic or social reasons, so that large investments and long lead times are required before reserves can be converted to marketable ore. Only countries with large consumption requirements can afford such an investment. Since the nuclear fuel cycle serves no purpose other than the generation of nuclear power, and since it cannot easily be converted to or from other industrial uses, a certain inflexibility is inherent in its adoption. Before a nuclear facility is built or the technology developed, a good load factor must be assured if the initial investment is to be recovered. Moreover, some of the facilities in the fuel cycle require a considerable service load. A reprocessing plant of 1,000-tons-per-year capacity would serve about 40 power plants of 1,000 MW_e (Megawatts electric) class, whereas a large gaseous-diffusion/enrichment plant can provide replacement fuel for ninety such

reactors. With gas-centrifuge technology, the scale of the individual plants may be smaller, but centrifuge-machine production capacity would probably still require about the same number
of 1,000 MW$_e$ plants as a service area, though the detailed
economics would, of course, vary according to machine designs.

In view of these characteristics, it is natural that the nuclear fuel-
cycle industry be organized on an international basis, with a
limited number of technology centers serving the needs of the entire world. There are at present three such centers—the United
States, the Soviet Union, and Europe—with Japan preparing to
take the fourth position. These centers each possess a range of
technological capabilities relating to uranium enrichment, fuel
reprocessing, plutonium fuel fabrication, light-water reactor
manufacturing, and development work toward commercialization
of the fast breeder. The three major centers happen also to be areas
with nuclear weapons capabilities. The major nonproliferation
issue of the day may thus be restated as follows: are we going to
limit the world's fuel-cycle technology to these three centers and
exert political pressure toward denying other regions an equal
status? To do so would be a mistake: three centers are too few to
meet the nuclear power demands beyond the year 2000.

Moreover, each of the three existing centers has certain short-
comings. As a supply center, the United States lacks credibility.
Other nations have become accustomed to the frequent changes in
U.S. policy concerning enrichment services and the use of
plutonium. Confusion in U.S. governmental and industrial circles
has left the Americans unable to agree on a coherent central policy.
The future of its reactor industry is also somewhat in doubt,
because of the prolonged lack of new plant orders.

U.S. commitments to supply enough enriched uranium to meet
the world's needs are unrealistic because the United States
possesses neither the required enrichment capacity nor the
necessary reserves of uranium ore. Nor do proposals to receive irradiated reactor fuel from outside the United States sound realistic,
since the disposition of spent fuel and radioactive waste are the
issues that have made it so difficult to license reactors even *within*
the United States. Moreover, the other nations of the world are
quite aware that the United States, with its abundant reserves of
uranium and coal, can survive until the year 2000 without resort-
ing to the use of plutonium as fuel. A nation for which nuclear

power may not be an ultimate need is bound to see its credibility as a supplier suffer.

The Soviet Union presents rather a different case. Although the Soviets have entered into several important supply arrangements with non-Communist countries, and have so far consistently honored all their commitments, the USSR refuses to reveal its service capacities, construction programs, or even the location of its fuel-cycle facilities. In contracting for Soviet-supplied services, many countries now look upon the Soviet Union chiefly as part of a diversification strategy and look with caution upon increasing their level of dependence on that source.

The European community, of course, is not a single entity. The United Kingdom, France, and West Germany have diverse nuclear interests and different levels of technological development; one of the three is not a nuclear weapons state. Economic conditions in the three countries are such that the construction of new fuel-cycle service facilities requires of its foreign users both capital subscription and participation in risk-sharing. For countries or regions with a sufficient service load, it makes more sense to build their own facilities than to depend on the European community, except perhaps for a transition period during which the service load gradually accumulates.

To apply political pressure to limit such technology centers to the nuclear weapons states alone would be to violate the spirit of the Nonproliferation Treaty, if not the letter of its provisions. Those who subscribed to the NPT accepted unequal status by recognizing, in the interest of global stability, five states as the holders of a monopoly on nuclear weapons. In return, the weapons states pledged to implement nuclear arms control and eventual disarmament. The nonweapon states also received an assurance that they would be free to develop nuclear energy for peaceful purposes. Watching the slow progress of nuclear arms control, as well as an actual escalation of the nuclear arms race, has been frustrating enough for the nonweapon states that ratified the NPT. To require now that the weapons states also be given monopoly rights to the fuel-cycle technology — again in the name of nonproliferation — will be seen as breach of contract. Any attempt to limit the nonweapon states' access to fuel-cycle technology by linking Article IV of the NPT with Article I will prove to be a futile, Orwellian attempt to control history; such a move can only breed distrust, and any erosion of the basic trust underlying the NPT will pose a serious threat to the cause of nuclear nonproliferation.[1] Since the economic and technical qualifications for becoming another technology center are possessed by only a few countries with a genuine need and ability to develop the plutonium option, it should be made a fundamental part of any comprehensive non-proliferation policy that those who qualify be permitted, indeed encouraged, to add to the fuel-cycle services available to the world.

The Problem of Technology Transfer

It is a long-standing tradition of the scientific community that discoveries of scientific value be freely published. Exceptions have been made where information of direct military value has been involved, and exceptions have been made when the research has been government funded. Those countries that publish more than their share of scientific articles have never been known to complain that this imbalance places them at a disadvantage internationally.

When a technology yields applications promising immediate profit, licensing arrangements involving royalties or other payments are common. One variation, employed chiefly where the development of the technology takes considerable time, is cooperative research and development. This category of technology transfer may be manifested in basic patents or in more practical know-how. The advantages and disadvantages of this form of technology transfer are increasingly debated. It is argued that, given the high cost and considerable risk of failure involved in the development of a new technology and the buildup of expertise, the monetary returns to the developer are insufficient, compared to what the recipients of technology transfer save in development costs, time, and risks. Thus, besides seeking a monetary return on his investment, the provider of the technology often demands control over the global marketing of his product. International joint ventures, with one party providing the technology and the other the capital, have not been uncommon.

Another form of technology transfer involves the direct sale of goods. This occurs when, for example, the United States sells its modern conventional weapons to the Middle East countries and provides follow-up service in the form of expert advice, pilot training, and supply of component parts.

When the United States was the world's lone supplier of nuclear technology, it could effectively restrict the international transfer of this technology. Today, with three centers of nuclear technology competing against one another for commercial advantage, technology transfer cannot so easily be restricted. History shows that commodity embargoes are difficult to sustain when an alternate supplier is at hand, especially if it is to the immediate economic or political advantage of the second supplier to make the sale, and if the good in question is of vital importance to the purchaser. The international transfer of technology has become a basic feature of the world economy during the present era; moreover, it is inevitable that those who possess scientific and technical knowledge will seek its wider use, either in order to compensate their investment, or to assure themselves a market large enough to sustain the integrity of their high-technology enterprise. Given these fundamental facts with respect to the transfer of technology, it is questionable whether the proliferation threat as defined by the United States will provide a sufficient basis for persuading nations with diverse interests to join in and sustain a selective embargo on nuclear technology. More specific discussion of objectives and compensatory arrangements will be needed.

Changing Views on the Role of Big Science

The successful conclusion of the Manhattan Project showed that an organized national effort to solve scientific and engineering problems could produce impressive results. From this experience developed a mentality that looked upon any scientific or engineering problem as solvable, given sufficient organization and scale. Science was believed capable of doing practically anything. In time, however, people came to realize that science and technology had grown so large and powerful as to seem often beyond human control. The revelations concerning the hazards of the insecticide DDT played a major role in bringing people to this realization, and environmental pollution has become an important concern in many nations. The unlimited escalation of the nuclear arms race produces better methods to kill more people, leaving many with a sense of despair, wondering whether it is already too late to curb the march of science and technology. Many now recognize that countries capable of sending men to the moon and returning them safely can nonetheless harbor gross social injustice. Man's view of Big Science clearly has undergone a rather drastic shift.

How all this relates to nuclear nonproliferation may not be immediately apparent. The relationship lies in the fact that people have come to feel much less restraint in rejecting the claims of the scientific community concerning what is necessary to achieve further advances. It is important to realize, however, that this kind of criticism of science and technology, like the philosophy of zero growth, is regarded by most of the world as a luxury to be contemplated only by the advanced industrial nations.

The Political Atmosphere of Détente

This is not the place to develop a sustained argument about the impact of superpower détente on the world order. Two points are sufficient. First, though there are but two superpowers in the military sense, the international political and economic order is far more decentralized and dissatisfactions with the world order are today freely expressed. Second, the easing of external tensions encourages the expression of domestic dissent, as well as attacks on the national leadership for its alleged mismanagement of international affairs. The world has entered an era in which it is easy, even fashionable, to criticize and very difficult to offer workable solutions. Some energy-related aspects of a world thus in flux will be further considered in Chapter 5.

Notes

1. Article I reads as follows: "Each nuclear-weapon State Party to the Treaty undertakes not to transfer to any recipient whatsoever nuclear weapons or other nuclear explosive devices or control over such weapons or explosive devices directly, or indirectly; and not in any way to assist, encourage, or induce any non-nuclear-weapon States to manufacture or otherwise acquire nuclear weapons or other nuclear explosive devices, or control over such weapons or explosive devices."

Article IV stipulates that: "Nothing in this Treaty shall be interpreted as affecting the inalienable right of all the Parties to the Treaty to develop research, production and use of nuclear energy for peaceful purposes without discrimination and in conformity with articles I and II of this Treaty. All the Parties to the Treaty undertake to facilitate, and have the right to participate in, the fullest possible exchange of equipment, materials and scientific and technological information for the peaceful uses of nuclear energy. Parties to the Treaty in a position to do so shall also cooperate in contributing alone or together with other States or international organizations to the further development of the applications of nuclear energy for peaceful purposes, especially in the territories of non-nuclear-weapon States Party to the Treaty, with due consideration for the needs of the developing areas of the world." From *Arms Control and Disarmament Agreements*, Texts and History of Negotiations (Washington D.C.: Arms Control and Disarmament Agency, 1975), pp. 86-87.

3

What Kinds of Proliferation Should Be Prevented?

Much as people may agree on the importance of nonproliferation, it is almost amusing to see how variously they define what
should be kept from proliferating. Depending on how the problem is defined, preventing proliferation may in fact be a physical
impossibility. This confusion about definitions seems especially
great in the United States, where it has led to the advocacy of
methods completely unsuited to the stated goals.

Targets of Nonproliferation Efforts

Logically, nonproliferation efforts should be directed at three
possibilities: (1) the potential for the production of crude nuclear
weapons; (2) the actual production of these weapons; and (3) the
production and deployment of deliverable nuclear weapons. The
success of the prevention efforts will be measured against one of
three basic outcomes: (1) nuclear weapons have been ruled out
decisively; (2) there is a reasonable assurance that nuclear weapons
will not be developed; or (3) the inevitable acquisition of nuclear
weapons has merely been delayed. Theoretically, then, there are
nine possible combinations of effort and outcome. The selection of
any particular combination as a national goal, vis-à-vis other
nations' goals, will be determined by the level of perceived threat,
social factors, and the extent of the nation's need for nuclear
power. It will also be affected by how the nation regards its ability
to influence the course of world history. We should remember that
the level of threat is measured against the proliferation of nuclear
weapons abroad, whereas nuclear power needs are chiefly a

domestic concern. Since countries define their nonproliferation objectives differently, an international consensus on nonproliferation policy is difficult to achieve. It will be useful to analyze some of the basic components of the traditional U.S. approach to nonproliferation, and then to see how approaches might differ under other conditions.

Whereas the United States has always viewed vertical and horizontal proliferation as separate phenomena, other countries have disagreed. In any hands, nuclear weapons are a hazard. In the United States, vertical proliferation — pitting the Trident or MX missiles or the B-1 bomber against the Soviet SS-18 or the SS-N-8 missiles, and the Tomahawk cruise missile against the Backfire bomber — is continuing in the name of national defense. And by now, of course, the nuclear warheads and delivery systems already possessed by the United States and the Soviet Union are infinitely more dangerous — to the entire world — than the nuclear weapons that some presently nonnuclear nation may produce in the future. The U.S. position — vertical proliferation with horizontal nonproliferation — can be justified only if the world accepts the notion that God has made a special arrangement on behalf of the United States, and the U.S. nuclear weapons will therefore be deployed (and used?) only for the good of the world. The world has certainly not accepted that notion. Thus any nonproliferation proposal that gives the weapons states special status in *peaceful* nuclear technology as well will be most vigorously rejected.

Traditionally, the United States has been free from any direct external threat to its national security. Its response to perceived threat tends to be massive and willful, as was demonstrated at the time of the 1949 Soviet atomic bomb test, or in the days of the Cuban missile crisis, and was evident in the somewhat baffling logic used to justify the development of a Safeguard antiballistic missile (ABM) system to counter Chinese ICBMs. Many countries, of course, have been living with much more direct threats. The nations of central Europe have lived under the constant strain of contemplating the prospects for all-out nuclear war. Japan has faced the perennial prospect of shortages in vital natural resources, and thus the possibility of rapid national economic collapse. These threats, offered simply as examples, are perceived as acute and immediate; they are at least as worrisome as the somewhat distant possibility that a neighboring country has come upon several crude nuclear explosive devices. The latter situation would of course be exceedingly unwelcome, but it is by now conventional wisdom that countries with nuclear devices will not use them against others unless they have themselves become truly desperate about the prospects for their own national survival. The United States, as many have recognized, tends to exaggerate potential threats, perhaps because of its preoccupation with scenario-based analysis of its own national defense.

The Americans also seem unaware of the weight of U.S. military experience in shaping overall U.S. attitudes on nuclear matters. Weapons-related activities, involving a great many employees, take up a good part of the federal nuclear budget; these activities produce tons of weapons-grade material every year, as well as many thousands of nuclear warheads of various configurations and kilotonnage. This is a phenomenon that people in other countries cannot truly appreciate. Because the development of nuclear weapons has such a long history in the United States, and because of the American desire to maintain a nuclear arsenal unsurpassed by any other nation, a unique culture has grown up around nuclear technology in the United States. Today, U.S. government leaders are instinctively incapable of thinking or acting without being influenced by that culture.

Thus, under the terms of the Energy Research and Development Administration's "Master Plan" of 1976, safeguards were originally conceived as a means of protecting the U.S. public against mishaps resulting from this weapons culture. The United States would do well to realize that no other country except the Soviet Union shares such a culture. In most countries, people engaged in nuclear activities do not automatically think of weapons nor do they come to that work from weapons experience, as is the case in the United States. It is also important to realize that countries lacking the technical sophistication possessed by a single MIT graduate do not expect to have to deal with hijackers capable of designing bombs and finding the necessary components in the corner drugstore. It is one thing to design a bomb, and quite another to build it. Anyone in the United States with experience in weapons technology will attest to the fact that nuclear weapons manufacture is far from being a backyard operation. In many countries, moreover, private ownership of firearms is illegal, and an attack on nuclear facilities by gangs armed with submachine guns is inconceivable. The U.S. definition of the nuclear proliferation threat is very much a product of conditioning peculiar to the United States.

Types of Proliferation

If the threat of nuclear proliferation is defined as the possibility that nations with access to nuclear technology may someday come up with a crude explosive device or two, there is nothing that can be done to prevent it. Knowledge of nuclear science and technology has already spread too far; what has happened cannot be undone. The problem then becomes a matter of degree—of restricting the further spread of nuclear technology and material. To guarantee that the presently nonnuclear nations will not acquire the potential to develop nuclear weapons would be tantamount to asking the nations of the world to forgo thinking about nuclear power as a source of energy; and even if such a consensus were reached, it would be too late. The *principles* of nuclear technology are already widely available, and the only meaningful goal under the present circumstances is to delay what is intrinsically unavoidable by providing a reasonable assurance that *sensitive details* of technical know-how will not unnecessarily spread into areas where there is no technical or economic justification for them. The lack of technological or social infrastructure alone is sufficient reason for denying transfer of sensitive details, which, after all, are not the first order of business for a nation that wishes to use nuclear energy for the generation of electricity or for other industrial purposes. In this sense "the nuclear proliferated world" is not unlike some other doomsday stories of population explosion or a thoroughly polluted environment. These scenarios serve as useful warnings but do not represent likely futures.

The next level of proliferation is the actual construction of crude explosive devices. If the problem of "potential" has been dealt with separately, then it is possible to focus on a practical analysis of diverting nuclear material to weapons use. Such an analysis leads to the conclusion that using a light-water reactor power plant to obtain reactor-grade plutonium may be the least attractive way of proceeding. More efficient would be to obtain either weapons-grade plutonium for critical experiments, or highly enriched uranium for research reactors, and then to divert from there. It is well known that uranium-based bombs are much easier to make than those based on the plutonium technology. It is thus crucially important to ensure that such materials are not transferred in the absence of absolute justification. Many people have pointed to the research facility as the place where IAEA safeguards should be more vigorously applied. The history of IAEA safeguards, as well as the statements of those in the nuclear bureaucracy, indicates that there has been rather too much concern for the safeguarding of light-water reactor plants or low enriched uranium fuel shops, and insufficient attention to loose weapons-grade material in research facilities.

It is time-consuming to construct and operate a nuclear power plant; the same is true of commercial reprocessing. Except in the case of "potential-hunting," this is not the recommended approach to proliferation. The more traditional approach taken by India, which cannot be justified given existing economic and tech-nological conditions, was to use the high-purity material produced by research facilities. Very uneconomical, but efficient, centrifuge machines could be used, and highly enriched uranium might be available from their operational testing; even that approach would be more economical and less time-consuming than reliance on power reactors. Although an explanation may be found in the pro-visions of the relevant treaties, it is nevertheless ironic that IAEA safeguards were placed on power reactors in India but not on the research-scale production reactor and the accompanying plutonium-extraction facility.

Although IAEA safeguards are not intended to prevent the pro-liferation of a long-term *potential* to build nuclear weapons, they can do a great deal to provide reasonable assurance that countries are effectively deterred from diversionary activities in the near term. IAEA safeguards are currently based on a probabilistic analysis of nuclear material accounting and of the containment of nuclear material; their purpose is to provide early detection of diversion. They are not intended to *prevent* diversion, and they cannot ensure absolutely the *detection* of all diversion possibilities, however remote or unlikely. Given the work that has been done in analyzing detection probabilities and detection time in relation to the characteristics of the fuel cycle in a given nation, IAEA safeguards can be made a reasonable instrument of a nonproliferation regime. An effort currently in progress seeks to reorganize safeguards into a credible deterrence system, not only in *diversion* cases but against weapons-oriented activities in general, and I am convinced that such a system can be made to work, except under unreasonable and unrealistic assumptions.[1] I shall return to the problem in considering the open-endedness of concerns about proliferation.

What Is a Meaningful Nuclear Weapon?

Experts have known for some time that a device using reactor-grade plutonium can explode. They also know that such a device is unreliable, that its yield is uncertain, and that its reliability deteriorates over time. Inherently, such a device is a poor prospect for deployment. With the highly advanced weapons technology of the United States or the Soviet Unioin, of course, a plutonium bomb is another matter. But the first device produced from this kind of material, by a country new to the technology, would be a crude one indeed.

The impact of such a device would be mostly psychological. A crude device is likely to be fairly large, and therefore unfit for-delivery by air. Given its unreliability, the device would fail to qualify as a weapon in the usual sense of the word. Successful underground testing (nowhere else is to be contemplated!) would allow the nation to claim that it dares to challenge the existing world order, that it is capable of acting in defiance of the great powers. The impact of such an achievement should never be underestimated, but it is doubtful that such a device would have any other effects. It would have almost no direct military significance, and thus would pose no direct threat to anyone.

Although it would be far better had the country been prevented from acquiring its device, since there is always some chance that the national leadership will be insane enough to contemplate actual military application, it is quite doubtful that the entire industrial world should be expected to sacrifice an important energy option to prevent it. The kind of political defiance that led to the bomb's construction could be much more effectively dealt with by maintaining an appropriate political climate, and by leaving no doubt, in advance, that this kind of adventurism will cost its perpetrators very dearly. If the country is nonetheless willing to pay the price, there is no effective way to stop it, regardless of refinements that may be made in nonproliferation procedures.

To be militarily significant, a nuclear device would have to meet minimum standards of effectiveness—including reliability of detonation and of yield, deliverability by air against significant air defenses, and replicability, if only at a very low rate. If all this is to be achieved, a way would have to be found to make the weapons small, and the nation would need to be equipped with modern fighter-bombers or high performance missiles. In this regard, restraints on the international sale of airplanes and missiles would be at least as important a nonproliferation measure as the export of critical nuclear technology. Although it may be arguable whether the delivery of a squadron of modern fighter-bombers is more or less significant than the export of several kilograms of weapons-grade nuclear material, the fighter-bombers are more directly related to the deployment of meaningful nuclear weapons than power reactors would be. The argument that fighter-bombers are a *stabilizing* weapon, whereas nuclear technologies are *destabilizing*, seems dubious at best.

Even should a country possess the minimum credible weapons system and delivery capability, does it really constitute a significant threat? It would certainly be disturbing politically to have such a neighbor, especially if it sought to use its nuclear weapons as leverage with which to extract political or economic gains. But actually to use the weapons would be insane. It would violate the first principle of nuclear weapons doctrine—namely, that nuclear weapons are useful primarily as a means of deterrence and must be employed with extreme care so as not to invite preemptive strikes or counterattacks. There is no reason to believe that the leaders of a new nuclear power would be so irrational; they would realize, in short order, that as a country with a small nuclear arsenal, their adopting an offensive posture would expose the country to greater danger than its nuclear weapons can prevent. They would realize, as well, that it is in their national interests to refrain from employing the weapons even for purposes of political threat. Their restraint, ironically, would serve to increase the political prestige of the country and its weight in international affairs. That outcome may be undesirable from the point of view of the great powers, but it does not portend the doomsday that is often associated with nuclear proliferation. The problem is not unmanageable, but other ways of garnering international prestige should be encouraged.

The Open-Endedness of Concern about Proliferation

International discussions of the effectiveness of IAEA safeguards over the last ten years have constantly been impeded by open-ended arguments. Safeguards are essentially a defensive tactic: those who wish to acquire nuclear weapons are free to choose the time and the place to start the exercise, and the defensive side must be alert to any eventuality. Whatever defensive scenario might be considered, it is always possible to conjure up some offensive scenario, however unrealistic, that can foil the defense. One of the more absurd scenarios envisioned a diverter who penetrated the wall of a reactor building (concrete two meters thick) and then carried off an irradiated fuel assembly containing millions of curies of radioactivity, enough to cause the instantaneous death of the carrier. If safeguards must cope with such extreme cases, there is no alternative but to place IAEA inspectors on twenty-four-hour watch everywhere. Even this would not suffice, because one could then raise questions about the integrity of the inspectors. Experts on safeguards agree that it is impossible to secure continuous knowledge of the status of nuclear materials, even at plutonium-producing or -handling facilities. The ultimate question, of course, is how effectively the international community can prevent the manufacture of weapons even when a diversion has been detected beyond doubt. That is clearly a political, not a technical, problem.

The absurd extremes of open-endedness that develop from these arguments are similar to some of the extremes in arguments made about nuclear safety. If a light-water reactor system must be designed so that even an accident that might occur only once in a million years is prevented with certainty, engineering has no effective means of complying with such a requirement except to refrain from building nuclear power plants at all. In this case, the technical arguments have been carried to such excesses that the original purpose of the exercise has been forgotten. Even with the level of safety design required today, light-water plants are suffering from the occasional breakdown of components whose function is defense against post-accident events. The probability of breakdown in the excessively sophisticated safety systems is a million times higher than the real accident probability. Current arguments about nonproliferation, as they are stated in some quarters in the United States, are so preoccupied with improbable scenarios that they have become ends in themselves, though making no useful contribution to the cause of nonproliferation.

It is important to add that this trend is by no means limited to the concerns of nonproliferation. Many of the arguments about environmental pollution are pursued in the same fashion. Indeed, this open-endedness is a problem evident in more general discussions concerning the effects of science and technology on society, especially when probabilities and scopes of adverse effects cannot be defined from past human experience.

Notes

1. Ryukichi Imai, "Basic Structure of Nuclear Nonproliferation Logic and the Role of Safeguards," paper under discussion by the Standing Advisory Group on Safeguards Implementation, IAEA.

4

In Search of Workable Solutions

One may question the wisdom of U.S. policy at the time the Atoms for Peace program was established twenty years ago, but that will not change the situation today. The fact remains that a considerable amount of nuclear technology has become public knowledge, and the concentration of research and development efforts on nuclear power has brought it much closer to industrial feasibility than any of the other new energy alternatives. It is contrary to the nature of science and technology to think that a handful of countries can retain a monopoly over an important technology for very long. If restraints were to have been established, the time to do it was in 1943, when the atomic bomb project was begun, or again in 1949, when a national program to develop the hydrogen bomb was approved despite strong opposition from some scientists.

The Search for Reasonable Assurances

Any attempt to eliminate all possibility of more countries developing nuclear weapons would mean doing away with a major sector of the nuclear industry. This is not only impractical but also clearly unacceptable to many countries that are concerned about energy supply. As they see it, to forgo the plutonium option (and the energy it could produce) today would pose a greater threat to national security in the decades to come than would the crude nuclear weapons that might be developed ten to fifteen years hence. It will take that long to construct a nuclear power plant, place it in operation, reprocess the spent fuel, and extract enough plutonium to build a crude nuclear weapon.

Uranium, as it naturally occurs, contains only about 0.7 percent of the fissionable U-235 atom while 99.3 percent of the remainder is U-238, which does not fission unless converted in reactors to a new element, plutonium. The importance of the plutonium option is illustrated by figures that describe the efficiency of energy use from the same amount of uranium ore under varying conditions. A light-water reactor without plutonium recycle makes use of 0.5 percent of the potential energy of the uranium. If plutonium is recycled in the same system, efficiency rises to 0.71 percent. Increasing efficiency from 0.5 percent to 0.71 percent is very significant, a 40.0 percent improvement. The saving is important for countries lacking uranium resources (though one might also point out that 0.96 percent efficiency is achievable in certain heavy-water reactor systems without relying on plutonium). By contrast, the fast breeder reactor without plutonium recycle gives 0.43 percent efficiency, whereas recycling raises efficiency to better than 90.0 percent (all figures assume 0.3 percent enrichment tail). The maximum utilization of potential energy in U-238 is possible only when a fast breeder with the plutonium recycle mode is adopted. This is the reason why the reactor for such a purpose is called a breeder. The proposal to abandon the fast breeder reactor is tantamount to a decision to forgo an important technical option, one with the potential to yield a practically unlimited supply of energy. Those who are unfamiliar with the industrial world must bear in mind that the development of an industrial technology calls for a good deal more than demonstrating that technology in the laboratory. Many years and many failures precede the actual operation of large-scale plants, and it is only in the course of such an enterprise that a group of really capable and experienced engineers is assembled within the industry. The nuclear weapon states already possess such capabilities because of their long experience in military plutonium production; the nonweapon states do not.

It is generally recognized that countries already in possession of advanced nuclear technology can build a meaningful nuclear arsenal, given concerted effort and financial commitment. That last qualification is of course the clincher: the technology of plutonium extraction or of uranium enrichment is not too difficult for such countries, *if they are not concerned about cost*. But countries now in possession of nuclear technology have *not* started on the path to nuclear armament and will not do so because the risks and political costs involved are too great and the potential military gains too dubious. If these assumptions are correct, only a very general application of international safeguards—perhaps only a means of detecting anomalies in national nuclear activities—should be sufficient to provide reasonable assurances against proliferation.

The rational approach to limiting arms acquisition by the technologically less developed countries is not to provide absolute assurances against remote potentialities, but to delay the more direct potentialities by concentrating—in a small number of highly secure service centers around the world—those nuclear fuel-cycle activities that employ sensitive technologies and materials. Since the economics of the nuclear fuel cycle dictate that uranium enrichment, spent-fuel reprocessing, and the development of plutonium technology can occur only in countries with advanced industrial technology and a very large-scale nuclear program, the less developed countries should be discouraged from contemplating these activities. This goal may be accomplished in two ways: by restricting the export of the relevant technology and materials, and by offering credible assurances that to the extent they are needed the necessary services and fuel supply will be provided. In any case, very few of the less developed countries have an immediate interest in these undertakings; the scale of economics in plutonium technology is sufficient demonstration that it is a realistic option for only a few countries.

It is important that IAEA safeguards on the nuclear facilities of these service centers provide assurances that the sensitive material will remain inside, but research facilities that employ weapons-grade material should be subject to equally vigorous safeguarding, so that abnormal handling of this material cannot be explained away in the name of research. Since research facilities provide easier and more practical access to weapons-grade materials, it is imperative that safeguarding measures concentrate on this area. Furthermore, given the present state of nuclear technology, it is unlikely that research activities in less developed countries can make any important contributions, and the application of strengthened safeguards would not jeopardize the conduct of research in such countries.

Besides these technical measures, there are three others that deserve attention, none of them deriving from the state of panic that so often plagues approaches to the proliferation problem. First, we must think about political and social means of removing incentives to develop nuclear weapons. Effort should be made to create an ambience in which potential proliferators do not feel compelled to defy (with nuclear explosions) the wishes of the industrially advanced nations. Second, it is important that the potential proliferators understand in advance the political, economic, and other costs of violating the nonproliferation code. This does not necessarily mean invoking prearranged international sanctions, which are usually very slow in coming and are often ineffectual, for these costs to the proliferator do not cease after the initial nuclear explosion has occurred. Rather, countries that have taken that first step should be made to realize that if they proceed to develop a more meaningful nuclear weapons system, additional, massive costs will be incurred. Finally, the weapons-exporting countries should be aware that the spread of conventional weapons systems capable of delivering nuclear bombs is at least as significant a step toward nuclear proliferation as the export of sensitive nuclear technology and material.

If we allow the discussion of nonproliferation measures to be open-ended, it will bear no fruit. Such discussions may help to define the boundaries beyond which further debate becomes meaningless, but the pursuit of scenarios that are absurdly unrealistic, even if technically consistent, can only antagonize the discussants. "Absolutely no proliferation at any cost" is an absolutely unachievable goal, a bankrupt national or international policy objective.

Discrimination, Not Universality

The preceding discussion demonstrates that the focus of the nonproliferation issue will differ from one country to the next, depending on whether the particular country is technologically advanced, less advanced but with a justifiable need for nuclear activities at some level, or less advanced but with a demonstrated, if largely symbolic, interest in nuclear power. It is unreasonable to assume that the same set of nonproliferation measures could be applied effectively to all of these countries. Rather than the uniform application of universal critieria, what is needed is a more discriminatory approach, one that would apply measures and procedures according to cases. In fact, the application of uniform measures, to the advanced and the less developed countries alike, has effects that are themselves highly discriminatory.

U.S. attempts to devise universally applicable nonproliferation measures are frustrated by the fact that most other countries have problems and perceptions that differ from those of the United States. The tendency of the U.S. to insist, in a rather legalistic way, on universality of treatment through the application of a comprehensive set of policies to all countries—and then to shift the orientation of those policies abruptly—has caused considerable confusion about the real motivations of U.S. nonproliferation policy. What the United States may regard as a normal overhaul of policy following the inauguration of a new administration nevertheless constitutes an instability that cannot but do damage to the efficacy and credibility of the U.S. position abroad.

One area in which a more discriminatory approach is definitely recommended relates to IAEA safeguards. As already noted, the overall concern of safeguards should differ, depending on whether one is looking at a country for which a small number of nuclear explosives will make only a negative contribution to national security, or a country that regards the problem in a different light. As a practical matter, safeguards that are effective in countries with only small-scale nuclear facilities and no major fuel-cycle plants may be much less useful in an economically advanced nation with a larger flow of nuclear material throughout its fuel cycle. Part of the safeguard technology that relies on probabilistic analysis of nuclear material flow is technically limited, as becomes evident when the amount of material being safeguarded is very large: here, even a very small percentage in measurement error implies the possibility of a significant amount of material becoming unaccountable. Thus, the application of uniform technical standards in both less developed and industrially advanced countries will yield stringent controls in the former, dangerously lax controls in latter.

Rather than concentrating efforts on improving the accuracy of measurement with respect to very large nuclear complexes, it would be more meaningful to seek the kind of information that would describe the actual pattern of activity within a country's entire nuclear industry. In the context of efforts to maintain international control, the requirements of physical protection of nuclear facilities and material are similar to the requirements of safeguards. Requiring sovereign nations to exercise internal technical control against the possibility that special nuclear material might be illegally removed from legitimate locations partly corresponds to the safeguard requirement of containment and surveillance. In this sense, but only in this sense, it may be said that physical protection adds nothing new to the procedural requirements of international safeguards.

The establishment of nuclear technology centers at several points around the world is an inescapable step toward nonproliferation. It is also discriminatory, but in a way that ought to be found acceptable, both because it conforms naturally to the structure of the international fuel-cycle market and because it can be justified on both economic and industrial grounds. At the same time, to discriminate on the basis of nuclear weapons status would be a grave mistake. In the first place, existing nuclear weapons are as detrimental to the cause of nonproliferation as the still nonexistent weapons about which so much concern is expressed. In the second place, even appearing to give special status to the nuclear weapon states would be tantamount to making sport with the sincerity of those who elected to participate in the Nonproliferation Treaty, notwithstanding other options open to them. For some, it might even confirm suspicions that the United States has been pursuing a sinister grand scheme, first to promote a monopoly of nuclear weapons, then to extend that monopoly into the field of peaceful uses of nuclear power.

The development of international fuel-cycle centers should conform with the natural conditions of supply and demand, rather than the nonindustrial logic of the nuclear bureaucracy. Nonproliferation is a necessary goal, but it is quite foreign to the internal logic of the international fuel-cycle market. Various proposals for multinational reprocessing centers did not succeed because of their disregard for the commercial and political logic of the nuclear industry. There is much more involved in an international joint venture than theoretical calculations of optimum reprocessing costs; one must also consider the availability of financing, the quality of labor, and the political implications of reprocessing foreign fuel. Organizing a joint venture of multinational character without granting access to the technology involved is a difficult undertaking and defies the first principle of management. If investment opportunity is the only incentive offered in what is a high-risk, long lead-time business, people may not find it reasonable to participate. Nonproliferation policy should not dictate the organization of business but should stand aloof, so long as there is a basic assurance that its most fundamental requirements will be met. But should a situation arise in which certain less developed countries are unable to find the necessary fuel-cycle services and see no viable alternative except to provide those services for themselves, then the United States might want to consider providing supply assurances, even if the terms are not financially equitable. Especially under these circumstances, a U.S. guarantee should be made credible.

Removing Political Incentives for Proliferation

Nonproliferation is a political goal; as such, it relies on technology to achieve only what politics alone cannot.

West Germany, Japan, and India provide somewhat diverse examples of the interplay of technology and politics with respect to nonproliferaton. West Germany and Japan have found that militarily meaningful nuclear weapons are beyond their means, in terms of the economic, political, and security costs that would be incurred. Though they may be technologically and industrially capable of developing nuclear weapons, they recognize that to do so would be politically expensive and would contribute nothing to their defense. In both cases, the irrelevance of a national nuclear weapons capability derives largely from alliance relationships with the United States. For these countries, the acceptance of IAEA safeguards should be regarded as a symbol of their intent to eschew nuclear weapons, rather than as a step toward emplacement of instrumentation that is in itself capable of preventing the manufacture of the first crude nuclear explosive. India exemplifies the opposite case: here, political considerations propelled the country *toward* the development of nuclear weapons. Given the dates when the weapons program began and reactor and reprocessing plants became operational, by 1974 it was already too late to prevent that first nuclear explosion by technological means. It would seem that the timing of the Indian detonation was determined mainly by political considerations, that India was driven by the promise of heightened national prestige.

Despite the Indian example, if the leaders of other less developed nations challenge the superpower-dominated world order and defy the expressed wishes of the industrially advanced states by carrying out nuclear explosions, the decision to do so will not have been easily reached. Even more difficult for them will be to follow such a course if the same political objectives can be achieved by other means. Encouraging the less developed countries to seek other means of demonstrating heightened national prestige, while removing political incentives to resort to the forbidden route, should be considered at least as important as any procedural or technical arrangements for the international fuel-cycle industry. If leaders of less developed countries nonetheless feel that nuclear weapons are the only road to national security, then the industrial nations should mount a campaign to apprise them of the military risks that possession of nuclear weapons would entail, and simultaneously pursue all efforts for the maintenance of military stability in the region. This response will be more effective than a mere statement of nonproliferation policy. If a majority of the less developed countries come to feel that they can with impunity challenge the world order by acquiring nuclear weapons, then there is very little the industrially advanced nations can do about it. The problem is not simply a matter of nuclear proliferation.

It would be a mistake to emphasize the power of the nuclear arsenals of the superpowers and to offer a wider nuclear umbrella on the ground that this approach has proved successful with respect to West Germany and Japan. The situation in which the less developed countries find themselves today is very different from the situation during the period when East-West confrontation was the dominant fact of international life. There are today not many countries that feel threatened by the nuclear weapons of either the United States or the Soviet Union. In their efforts to advance the cause of nonproliferation, the superpowers can accomplish more by downplaying the usefulness of nuclear weapons than by extending nuclear protection to additional countries.

5
Systems Analysis
of Nonproliferation Logic

The chief criticism of recent U.S. nonproliferation policy has been that it managed to jeopardize the energy programs of the industrially advanced countries without offering viable alternatives. There is little likelihood that these countries, the major allies of the United States, will acquire nuclear weapons. The real proliferation danger lies with a class of less developed countries that are dissatisfied with the world order, whose technology and industry are expanding, and whose leadership has probably not thought through the implications of nuclear armament. The U.S. policy has succeeded only in providing the countries of the South with a pretext to announce the emergence of "new industrial and technological imperialism," without visibly reducing the risks of proliferation.

Looking Beyond a Confused World

In order to test that accusation, and to inquire how the situation might be rectified, we shall examine some of the major events in nuclear energy in the first two years after the initial Carter nonproliferation proposals and juxtapose these events against a world lapsing into confusion.

In September 1977 an agreement was reached between the governments of the United States and Japan regarding interim operation of the Tokai Mura reprocessing plant. According to Article 8-C of the U.S.-Japan Agreement for Cooperation on Peaceful Uses of Nuclear Power, the United States holds indirect right of approval regarding the reprocessing of spent fuel that contains

47

U.S.-supplied enriched uranium. After protracted and emotional negotiations, the two nations agreed that the plant will process up to ninety-nine tons of spent fuel within the interim two-year period. "Safeguardability determination," according to Article 8-C, has been interpreted in such a way that the mode of operation after the two-year period will be strongly influenced by the outcome of the International Nuclear Fuel Cycle Evaluation. The INFCE was instituted in October 1977 with more than forty nations and international organizations participating. Each of its eight working groups, with increasing numbers of subgroups and task forces, has been convening almost monthly, examining a wide range of issues, including world uranium supply, proposed mechanisms for supply assurance, proliferation-resistant technologies for plutonium use, the future of the fast breeder reactors, the processing and storage of spent fuel from light-water reactors, and alternative nuclear fuel cycles without plutonium.

Within the United States, Congress passed, and the president signed, in March 1978, the Nuclear Nonproliferation Act, thus mandating the administration to negotiate with the world at large, and the European Atomic Energy Commission (Euratom) countries (Belgium, Netherlands, Luxembourg, West Germany, France, Ireland, Italy, Britain) in particular, an agreement that would have them abide by the U.S. view of the future of nuclear power. In spite of legal wording that seeks to avoid the impression, the act is seen by many as an attempt to anticipate and preempt the major findings of the INFCE studies, which ought not to be available until the conclusion of the two years stipulated in the original plan for the studies. And because the president and Congress each have right of veto over the decisions of the other, many critics of the act complain that it is very difficult to know whom to negotiate with most seriously. (The three basic documents, the U.S.-Japan Tokai Mura Agreement, the Communiqué of the INFCE Organizing Conference meeting in Washington, and the U.S. Nonproliferation Act of 1978, are included in the Appendix.)

Perceptions of nuclear power as a means of satisfying the energy demand for the remainder of the twentieth century have been undergoing marked change during these two years. The outlook is becoming more confused, more uncertain, and opinions are sharply divided on the role of nuclear power, as well as on the timing and form of its use. An increasing number of environmentalists and advocates of "appropriate technologies," especially in the United States, would deny practically any role for nuclear power or, for that matter, for any form of "centralized hard technology" as a means of providing energy for the future of mankind. The ambivalence of U.S. energy policy on this issue has worked to further estrange the United States from the other industrialized countries, whose official policy has been to promote nuclear power, including its plutonium option. The handling of the Carter energy bill within the U.S. Congress through 1977 and 1978 did nothing to resolve this rift. The impression created is that the country of abundant natural resources can afford to continue its desultory debate on the energy question while increasing oil imports from a level of 6 million barrels per day in 1975 to 9 million in 1977 and possibly to 11 million by 1985, thus further endangering the already delicate balance of the world's oil supply and demand, as well as the stability of oil prices, during the coming years.

Since the 1973 oil crisis, the pattern of energy consumption in the industrially advanced countries has undergone marked change. Not only has growth in their GNP been much reduced from what they were accustomed to during the period of rapid economic growth in the 1960s, but the ratio of energy-consumption growth to GNP growth (energy elasticity) has been much smaller. Because of massive stagnation in the energy-intensive heavy industrial sectors, some countries are experiencing elasticity figures as low as 0.5, and the uncertain prospects for the world's economic recovery make forecast of demand in the 1980s extremely difficult. What the world is experiencing today cannot be described even with the most conservative extrapolation from the past. Widely held views about the pattern of industrialization among the less developed countries are also changing: it may no longer be feasible or even desirable to assume that they will pursue the path to industrialization in the manner once common among the countries of Western Europe or Japan and thus emerge as giant energy consumers by the turn of the century. In short, universal faith in the ability of big technology to work wonders is waning.

Uncertainties of supply are no less grave. The Middle East's unstable political and military relations, growing economic and social disparities, and general unrest make the region's oil-production capacity in the 1980s all the more unpredictable. The once-powerful seven major oil companies seem less confident of their continued role as distributors of crude oil and its products. Since the collapse of the Bretton Woods arrangements, the international monetary system has been unable to restore balance in the world's currencies, especially after the crucial perturbations caused by the fourfold increase in the price of oil. The resulting fluctuations in the world's confidence in the dollar, the governing currency of the postwar period, have brought on mounting apprehensions about the stability of international trade, including the oil trade. If the 1977 report of the Central Intelligence Agency proves to have been accurate and the USSR relinquishes its status as net exporter of oil for that of net importer by the middle of the 1980s, all are agreed that the shift will have profound effects on energy policies throughout the world. Work on alternative energy technologies has just begun, and none has yet produced convincing evidence of reliability as a significant contributor in the global energy picture. Even such semiconventional technologies as massive use of coal and comprehensive conservation measures have not proved their long-term feasibility. The outlook remains unchanged: only nuclear power, based on light-water reactors, promises the sort of industrial capacity that, if allowed to run its course, could substantially improve its contribution to energy supply—to better than 10 percent of total national energy requirements in the 1980s in many of the industrialized countries.

Against such a background, it is difficult to predict the future or to propose policies based on such predictions. In fact, fewer and fewer people are willing to make such predictions for fear of losing public credibility. Be it concerning the outcome of the INFCE exercise, the reactions of the less developed countries to nonproliferation proposals, or the energy supply-and-demand balance in the still primarily oil-dominated world of the 1980s, stating an opinion is too precarious a venture, except to reaffirm the uncertainties. The changes that are taking place are so rapid, and the pattern of their interactions so complicated, that it is sometimes difficult even to grasp correctly the changes themselves. It is, then, all the more important that we strive to understand the basic undercurrents, rather than to analyze and evalutate passing phases of the specifics. It is often said that three decades after World War II the world has entered into a period of flux and transition, a process that affects political, economic, military, technological, and cultural factors alike. And the issue of nuclear nonproliferation is simply one of these factors. When discussing the legal, political, technical, or procedural specifics of the current worldwide nonproliferation exercise, we should bear in mind the underlying pattern of global interdependence. To attach excessive importance to every sign of change is like building a house of cards on a foundation of quicksand.

Avoiding Popular Misconceptions

When faced with a set of equations, the mathematician has essentially two choices: he can look for general solutions that will satisfy the equations under any and all conditions; or he can work on specific solutions, i.e., the equations may be so difficult and their interrelationships so complicated that the best practical approach is to limit the problem to a set of specific boundary conditions. The physicist may find that the physical world is so complicated, and our understanding of it so shallow, that it is impossible even to define the entire set of equations. Rather than give up on the problem, he proceeds with a definition of equations for special and limited cases—Einstein's special relativity theory preceded his general theory of relativity. The series of nonproliferation proposals that the United States has presented since early 1977 looks like a general solution to an as yet undefined set of equations. It is natural, then, that the world would be baffled by them. Within the nonproliferation equations are *many* variables, not solely the consideration of whether a single nuclear weapon is acquired by somebody. Energy is another important variable; so are national prestige and technology transfer as a vehicle for economic development. Each of these additional variables commands its own set of complex equations; though the original Carter nonproliferation proposal had not worked the relationships out, it nonetheless made them the basis for a sweeping proposal, a panacea for the overall problem. Although the language of the proposal had the United States asking for time to think the problem through, it was evident that the basic value judgment had already been made.

To continue the analogy with the problem in physics, it is part of traditional wisdom to examine past attempts at attacking the problem and to seek the reasons why a satisfactory general solution has not been arrived at. The U.S. proposal of 1977, by contrast, has the earmarks of a solution worked out by people who had newly discovered the nonproliferation problem. Although the "energy crisis" had indeed led many to forget the crucial importance of nonproliferation, and although these people should be grateful for having been rudely reawakened, there are many who properly resent what to them appeared like neglect of all their past efforts.

Defining a set of equations for the problem of nuclear nonproliferation is a complicated process. To begin, we must define the nature of the problem. There are, roughly speaking, three different approaches. One is to define the problem as the technical one of preventing any possibility of someone's manufacturing a single nuclear explosive device; this would involve primarily the withholding of "risk" situations, such as the availability of weapons-usable nuclear material, weapons-manufacturing facilities, and know-how. This is not the place for technical details, but despite what is claimed by some of the do-it-yourself bomb stories, none of these three prerequisities for bomb production are easy to acquire. Two problems associated with this definition are that, in order to assess the risks properly and to cope with them, one must have fairly precise knowledge of nuclear explosive techniques; and that the "authority" who would exercise the necessary control must be defined.

The second approach to the problem focuses on the capability of government authorities to prevent the manufacture of nuclear explosives by subnational groups. This, of course, relates directly to the government's ability to maintain law and order domestically. This second approach calls not only for the technical measures of the first approach, but also for administrative procedures to define and prevent "unauthorized" manufacture of explosives. Strictly speaking, the second definition of the problem leaves room for the "authorized" manufacture of nuclear explosives by nation-states. Very often, people misunderstand nuclear nonproliferation in its international context because they assume the problem is merely one of extending such administrative controls to the international arena. They think the problem can be defined by distinguishing those states that are internationally authorized to engage in such activities (namely, weapon states) from those that are not (namely, nonweapons states). Some undefined international authority is expected to make the necessary distinctions and clarifications. Although the technical and administrative approaches are both important components of any comprehensive attack on the problem of international nuclear proliferation, a preoccupation with either or both of these approaches tends to obscure the central fact that, at bottom, the problem is political.

The third approach proceeds from a recognition that nuclear nonproliferation in the international context, like international relations generally, is basically a political matter. To prevent the number of weapon states from increasing, all the forces of international politics must be brought into play. It is the first lesson in international relations that consensus, not world government, is the engine of progress. Nations will have different notions of how to measure national prestige, perceptions of security threats, and conceptions of international justice. In the name of reaching consensus, these must often be compromised. Thus, in the search for effective control of international nuclear proliferation, the present five nuclear weapon states must expect to be asked why they should regard themselves as exceptions to the rule, and what they have done to minimize the risk of nuclear destabilization. To avoid these questions and pretend that the entire problem is either technical or administrative will only impede efforts to reach a solution.

Within the third approach one may further distinguish three different stages, as we saw in Chapter 3. The first is preventing access to sensitive nuclear technologies and materials in general. The second is preventing access to weapons-related potentials (or at least preventing their indiscriminate spread). The third is accepting the acquisition of potential but establishing assurances that to attempt to turn this potential into reality would incur for the violator unbearably high costs, political and otherwise. When a sovereign state has reached the considered judgment that acquiring the full range of nuclear technology is a vital option in national energy policy, only the second and third approaches are practicable, especially when the desire seems to be objectively justifiable. An institutional framework is needed to provide the necessary means of surveillance so that many weapons-oriented nuclear activities will be quickly discovered by the international community. It is also necessary to raise the costs of going nuclear and thus to reduce the political and other incentives for doing so. In reality, steps two and three must be combined to achieve the goal of nonproliferation.

Table 5.1 describes the logic of nonproliferation as it relates to existing realities. Although the three approaches are interrelated, they constitute different concepts. The third, in particular, cannot be described as a simple extrapolation from the other two. International discussion should therefore focus on *technical approaches* for the purpose of evaluating technical risks, *administrative procedures* for establishing national credibilities for nuclear material and technology control, and above all, the factors that determine the *political costs and benefits* of going nuclear.

The Emerging Pattern of Interdependence

If our initial position is to be that international nonproliferation is primarily a political problem, it is clear that our next consideration should be an investigation of those factors constituting the background and context of this issue in international politics. It is often argued that the basic pattern in international politics today is interdependence. In the world of decades past, a single construct, namely, "military power," was the guiding force in international relations. There are today other, equally important factors to be reckoned with. Energy and food are counted among the important factors. A different, but equivalent, perspective might offer technology, capital, resources, and information as the four dominant elements defining international relations today.

With the number of determining factors thus increased, relations between nations become more complicated, less direct, and perhaps more intimate, and the domestic and foreign policies of sovereign states are no longer separable. All of this is exemplified in current concerns about energy. In the past energy has been primarily an issue for domestic politics. No standard work that analyzes the role of energy in international politics is yet available. Because energy has so recently come onto the international stage, its role continues to be redefined.

1. Superimposed on the traditional East-West political polarity is the burgeoning North-South political and economic polarity and the proposed New International Economic Order, which came

Table 5.1
Three Approaches to Defining the Nonproliferation Problem

TECHNICAL:	PREVENTING THE MANUFACTURE OF A SINGLE NUCLEAR EXPLOSIVE DEVICE
Issues:	withholding weapons-usable materials, weapons-manufacturing facilities, and know-how
Problems:	amassing the detailed knowledge of explosive technology, and identifying the authority to be charged with the above listed responsibilities
Reality:	technically difficult unless the boundary conditions are clearly defined
ADMINISTRATIVE:	PREVENTING THE MANUFACTURE OF NUCLEAR EXPLOSIVES BY UNAUTHORIZED SUBNATIONAL GROUPS
Issues:	maintaining domestic law and order; establishing credible control mechanisms
Problems:	finding the optimum combination of technical and administrative measures
Reality:	dependent on the extent of social order achieved in a given society
POLITICAL:	BLOCKING INCREASES IN THE NUMBER OF NUCLEAR WEAPON STATES
Issues:	preventing general access to nuclear explosive potentials (equivalent to a denial of nuclear technology altogether); preventing access to weapons-related potentials (or at least preventing their indiscriminate spread); providing sufficient disincentives (both positive and negative) to the acquiring of nuclear armament
Problems:	tracking the interplay of many international political considerations, in an effort to distinguish those nations that are, or are not, qualified to use weapons-potential technology; providing sufficient compensation for forgoing such potentials (e.g., a credible international supply-guarantee regime); defining the "surveillance" and "disincentive" mechanisms
Reality:	prone to confusion of concepts with those of the other two approaches

more sharply into focus when the OPEC nations began to demonstrate their power over oil, the most critical of energy resources. All the related issues of military stability, political implications of military strength, and so on, were brought to the fore.

2. OPEC strength is very much conditioned by the future solidarity of the OPEC nations, much of which depends upon the congruence of economic interest among its members, and on the prospects for military stability in the Middle East.

3. The future balance of supply and demand in global energy is crucial. As has already been noted, the prospects for the 1980s have become markedly uncertain and the extent of uncertainty is governed by the possibilities for new non-OPEC oil finds, acceptable growth rates in the industrialized world, and so on. Availability of domestic energy resources, extent of optimism or pessimism about the new technologies, and nations' perceptions of their various abilities to influence international relations will provoke different responses: some countries will cling more strongly to the nuclear option, whereas others may incline toward non-nuclear options.

4. The modernization or industrialization strategies of the less developed countries will have a major impact on the world energy balance. If these states undertake modernization by turning immediately to import-substitution industries, energy elasticity could be very high, and as Wassily Leontieff has calculated in his U.N. study of 1977 (*The Future of the World Economy*), the rate of oil and gas consumption in these countries could be very high. That appears unlikely, but if, by the year 2000, worldwide oil-production capacity clearly cannot meet the combined requirements of the advanced and less developed countries, the latter may be amply justified in turning to expanded nuclear power programs to fill the gap.

5. Chronic shortages of capital and market capacity in the less developed countries have often been accompanied by industrialization efforts yielding a widening duality between urban elite and rural masses. It is widely and strongly felt that the pace of industrialization is too forced, that if it were more relaxed the so-called appropriate technologies could play a larger role. Where this view comes to dominate national planning, nuclear power will be eschewed, and to the extent that this view takes hold, nuclear technology need not proliferate into certain areas of the less developed world.

6. On the domestic front, in many of the advanced countries, is the issue of priorities in research and development, as well as competition between technological and social programs for limited national resources. Once a technology has been developed, recovering the investment through its sale abroad (technology transfer) becomes an issue. The problem will be exacerbated under the much more severe economic constraints of the 1980s. If such considerations were in the past part of the basis for the sale of modern conventional weapons to the resource-rich less developed countries by the United States and several West European countries, then the implications of an analogy with nuclear technology and the issue of nonproliferation should be clear.

7. A number of factors are taking their place alongside the demand and supply forecasts in any rational assessments of nuclear technology and nonproliferation: the unequal geographic distribution of energy resources and technology; the resulting problems of resource trade and technology transfer; objective analyses and subjective perceptions of national military security and of national goals and prestige; and the role of the international monetary system in controlling the flow of capital, goods, and services. For present purposes, two observations are sufficient.

First, because of the increasing number of dominant factors in international relations, a comprehensive, detailed description of the equations related to international nonproliferation is not possible at this time. If technology, resources, capital, and information are the four major factors in international politics, then how are we to assess nuclear nonproliferation, which is closely related to all four? And since nonproliferation is primarily a political affair, its description requires domestic as well as international equations.

Second, in the nonproliferation context the importance of the North-South relationship cannot be overemphasized. Although the advanced nonweapon states, whose primary concern is the maintenance of the basic world order, have discovered the uselessness of weapons acquisition for their national security, some of the less developed countries, whose preoccupation is to bring about changes in the status quo, seem to have a very different appreciation of this powerful means of challenging the world dominion enjoyed by the great powers. After all, this shift of potential incentives from North to South has been at the heart of the non-proliferation problem in the late 1970s.

8. Finally, nuclear power, like any other industry, cannot be undertaken on a viable basis below a certain scale of operation. For an industry based on light-water reactors, that scale is roughly 50 power stations of 1 GW_e each. That so large a scale is needed derives from the very capital-intensive and technology-intensive nature of this industry. Nuclear power is a highly sophisticated and therefore very expensive technology, a fact that has only become clear from the hard experience of recent years. If the illusion that *anyone* can effectively employ nuclear power is at the base of the belief that anyone has a right to acquire nuclear technology, a figure like 50 GW_e, the equivalent of the total electric power generating capacity of Canada or France today, may turn out to be the most persuasive argument on behalf of the nonproliferation proponents. We might add that to acquire the transfer of any technology, at any time, from abroad is not among the natural rights of a sovereign state.

Criteria for Risk and Threat Assessment

Before taking up the specific nonproliferation or proliferation-resistant measures currently under discussion in the INFCE forum, we will do well to clarify the criteria for their evaluation. The application of different sets of criteria to the problem can easily lead to very different conclusions and needless confusion.

There are those who believe that nuclear power is crucial to their future energy needs, but even among these people, opinions are divided on when and how it might best be incorporated into regional or national power systems. Some claim that unless the contribution of nuclear power is expanded immediately, the future of the world is doomed, whereas others insist merely on retaining the nuclear power option. Some assume a light-water reactor base well into the twenty-first century, whereas others insist it is imperative that the plutonium-based fast breeder reactor achieve large-scale operation before the end of this century. It is clear that reconciling energy-use requirements with proliferation concerns will demand compromise. Similarly, reconciliations with the safety and environmental effects of nuclear radiation will demand compromise. There is of course a broad spectrum of opinion on the magnitude of the risks involved, whether in proliferation potentials, safety hazards, or environmental effects.

At the same time, there are those who believe nuclear power is simply not necessary. By taking the arguments about proliferation, safety, and the environment to their absolute limits, they conclude that, regardless of the benefits that might derive from nuclear power, the nuclear option is no option at all. Any nonproliferation regimen is futile, since nuclear power has no proper role to begin with. There are also those who argue that world energy demand will decline, or that we shall find sufficient other means to supply the necessary energy levels.

It is only natural that these two groups—the powerhawks and the powerdoves—will come to very different conclusions from the same data and comparable reasoning. The fact that a totally accident-free technology is unrealistic leads one group to insist on banning all nuclear activities, whereas the same observation leads others to a serious discussion of "How safe is safe enough?" and to the conclusion that one should be prepared to establish a socially acceptable level of risk for any technology. Similarly, the difficulty of establishing absolutely foolproof technical safeguards on minute amounts of plutonium produces the argument that ensuring nonproliferation is the equivalent of banning the plutonium technology outright; that same difficulty leads others to seek through political means the weapons disincentives that will ensure dependable technical safeguard measures. The situation is exasperating, and we shall do well to recognize these two fundamentally different approaches. Since a good deal of the nonproliferation debate is an attempt to establish reasonable compromise or to optimize among conflicting requirements, those who have already repudiated the nuclear option, or who demand that nonproliferation take precedence over energy needs in any and all cases, cannot meaningfully contribute to the debate.

Optimization itself emerges in many guises. *Technical* optimization, for example, if pursued independently of other considerations, might say that the heavy-water reactor is the most effective means of burning uranium without the need for reprocessing the spent fuel. Similarly, the nuclear park, which combines plutonium extraction and plutonium fuel fabrication in one location, is the optimum technical solution to the problem of physical protection if reprocessing is required, because it minimizes the transportation of pure, separated plutonium. During the brief history of nuclear power, there have been many reactor concepts, fuel-cycle concepts, and the like that were optimized technically against different sets of contextual conditions. Indeed, the problem of optimization becomes more complicated when other considerations are introduced. For example, heavy-water reactors have not been subjected to as rigorous a safety evaluation as light-water reactors. Because heavy-water reactors require daily refueling with the reactor on load, they are more accessible for potential diverters. Safeguarding on-load-refuel reactors is notoriously difficult if one's major concern in safeguarding is the spent fuel. The heavy-water reactor produces an isotopic composition of plutonium much more suited to explosives production than the plutonium of light-water reactors.

Heavy-water production, moreover, requires the creation of a major new industry. Toward that end, what is sought is *industrial* optimization, because for any reactor or fuel-cycle concept to be feasible, it must be industrially viable — it must be a sound basis for the development and long-term operation of a large-scale industrial plant. It is well-known historical fact that the United States chose light-water reactors as the foundation of its nuclear-power program not because they constituted optimum technology — they do not — but because the vast experience of the U.S. navy with these reactors had made them the most obvious base to work from. With the lessons of the nuclear navy plus twenty years of industrial effort behind the light-water technology of today, the world's nuclear industry can ill afford to invest comparable amounts of time, money, and talent in bringing alternative industrial bases — the thorium reactor, the tandem fuel cycle, or the spectral-shift reactor — up to the proven dependability and scale of operation of the light-water base.

Choosing a technology can also be a process of *political* optimitization. The Shippingport reactor was built not because the United States needed the electric power it would generate, but rather to establish the prestigious postion of being first in nuclear power. Even if the United States were to claim today that Shippingport had been a mistake (it does not so claim), the United States cannot now deny other countries the freedom to optimize their choices of technology through a similarly suspect process.

Finally, although it may no longer be fashionable to talk about economic considerations in nuclear power, *economic* optimization is an unavoidable step. Seeking a return on massive investments in technological development through export is a familiar pattern; undertaking the development of a power industry based on a new fuel cycle may mean simply an expanded export drive. Nor is it difficult to imagine the situation in which nonproliferation constraints raise operating costs so high that the new technology, while still in the planning stage, is priced out of the market, vis-à-vis the more conventional energy technologies. Making the fuel for a fast breeder reactor inaccessible to a potential diverter through preirradiation may well rank among such economically nonoptimal solutions because of the enormous costs that would be involved in handling such irradiated fuel.

Nonproliferation, then, calls forth a highly complicated set of equations and often incompatible sets of criteria. A technically optimized solution for prolonging the life of the world's uranium resources, and thus forestalling the advent of the plutonium era, may be less than optimum from the point of view of safeguards. Techniques that are technically proliferation-resistant may in fact be economically prohibitive or industrially unrealistic, and here we have not "optimization" but the "no nuclear power" option. Although it is certainly not my purpose to confuse the argument, this much exposure to the context and patterns of nuclear power planning seems a necessary prerequisite to the examining of specifics. A proposal that looks optimum under one set of criteria may not stand a chance when other criteria are employed, and that dilemma is evidently endemic among the many ideas now being floated internationally.

6
Specific
Nonproliferation Proposals

Although not even a tentative international consensus is in sight regarding optimum nonproliferation measures, it will be useful to attempt an evaluation of the virtues of the several measures proposed, using the general framework of discussion offered in Chapters 4 and 5.

World Uranium Reserves

An important and familiar argument states that the world harbors much greater uranium reserves than are presently known and that a viable nuclear industry can be maintained by burning uranium in light-water reactors indefinitely—without, that is, having to convert to the plutonium-burning fast breeder system. If this projection is accurate, there is *no* need to reprocess spent fuel from light-water reactors and to extract plutonium. But this raises three problems.

1. By increasing the world's demand for uranium-enrichment services, we will inevitably spread the enrichment technology, and to do so is a greater proliferation risk than to burn plutonium, because enriched uranium—especially that extracted from light-water reactors—makes better bombs than does plutonium.

2. The claim is made that unprocessed spent fuel (from light-water reactors) stored in various parts of the world is a greater proliferation and safety risk than the reprocessing option.

3. More efficient use of uranium reserves will lead to heavy-water moderated reactors, which are free from enriched uranium, but at the same time, heavy-water reactors constitute a greater prolifera-

tion risk, as we have seen.

Whether there is enough uranium in the world to eliminate the need for plutonium is a difficult question. Everyone agrees that there must be a great deal more uranium in the world than is presently known. But from the point of view of energy policy, the following problems must be confronted:

a. For many mineral resources, including oil and nonferrous metals, exact reserve figures will never be known. There are many practical problems of investment, technology, and politics to be solved before potentials can become realities. National energy policies must be based on "what is," not on "what might be."

b. Uranium that might be discovered is quite a different matter from uranium that is directly available. The economics of uranium mining are such that guaranteed demand is required before the necessary high-risk, capital-intensive, long-lead-time investment can be undertaken. Because of the uncertainties surrounding nuclear power, no one is in a position to guarantee large-scale demand ten or fifteen years from now.

c. Uranium, like oil, is not a commodity of unregulated international commerce. Fluctuations in U.S. enrichment-service policy, the complete embargo of Canadian uranium in 1977, and the halt of uranium mining in Australia, all predicated on nonproliferation claims, have demonstrated that uranium and enrichment services are politically very sensitive.

Although the world uranium reserves may or may not prove to be sufficient for prolonged use of the light-water reactor, the proof will be in the pudding. Those who are asked to abandon the plutonium option as a national energy policy will take little comfort from predictions about uranium reserves.

International Fuel-Supply Guarantees

If abundant uranium reserves are not alone a persuasive argument, international guarantees to supply the necessary amounts of enriched uranium fuel are offered to convince the world that it need not pursue the plutonium path. This "bank" concept, circulating since the first days of the peaceful uses of nuclear power, confronts us with three basic difficulties.

1. To supply the projected demand of nuclear power, we are

talking about the fueling of 250 GW$_e$ by 1985, and 500 GW$_e$ by 1990, or substantial fractions thereof. The corresponding consumption of uranium would be 90,000 and 150,000 tons annually. A bank or network of banks sufficient to handle such amounts is not a viable proposition. More likely, the bank in question would serve only those countries with relatively small-scale nuclear power programs, which would otherwise find it difficult to secure the necessary uranium or uranium-enrichment services.

2. Since both uranium-ore extraction and enrichment-service capabilities are controlled by individual nations, the credibility of the bank guarantee must be determined by the extent of control the bank can exercise over, and sometimes against, the sovereign will of these states. It is almost inconceivable that some sort of international body could order a U.S. enrichment plant to supply service against the express wishes of either the U.S. administration or Congress. The existence of the Nonproliferation Act of 1978 makes this point quite clear, for it is precisely against shifts in national policy that the bank would be expected to protect its customers. The only meaningful way out of that dilemma would be for the bank to maintain its own substantial buffer storage, and this could be accomplished only if its service area were sharply limited and its commitments confined to a very few reactors.

3. How such a bank is to proceed toward equitable decisions is another delicate matter. If the decision-making process is established on a UN-type one-state, one-vote basis, the suppliers will be unhappy indeed, for they will be woefully outnumbered. If the choice is a structure of the World Bank (IBRD) type, with voting rights granted according to participating shares, the system could easily become dominated by the policies of the supplying countries, which runs counter to the bank's basic purposes. If only the supplying countries participate in the creation and direction of the bank, then the result is not different from the OPEC stranglehold on oil, which certainly does not constitute an international mechanism for supply guarantee.

That the bank concept distinguishes the "guaranteed" from the "guarantors" is seductively simple. Though the distinction may appear natural in the case of uranium ore, because the relationship is geographically dominated, it is not that simple, especially since most of the uranium-resource countries need foreign capital investment for exploration and development. In the case of uranium enrichment, which as a technology represents a considerable proliferation risk, the world will have to be divided between the *guarantors*, who are free to develop the technology and produce enriched uranium for both domestic use and bank-channeled foreign supply, and the *guaranteed*, to whom neither enrichment technology nor enrichment facilities are accorded. For although the argument for the bank is anchored in plutonium-risk consideration, it is clear that without limits on the enrichment-technology proliferation, the whole bank concept is self-defeating. Thus, what the bank implies is a neat division of the world into two camps, and the only way *that* can be avoided is to internationalize everyone's enrichment technologies and facilities along the lines of the old Baruch Plan. Not only is this unlikely, as the fate of that internationalization proposal back in 1945 attests, but it leaves unresolved the problem of decision making.

Reprocessing Now or Later

The age of the fast breeder reactor may be far down the road, or it may be just around the corner, and the world may need all the plutonium that can be extracted from the spent fuel of the light-water reactors. If the former case, is it preferable to store the spent fuel as is rather than reprocessing and storing the plutonium as a ready product? Safety and environmental concerns point both ways. As concerns proliferation resistance, some observers argue that dispersed storage of spent fuel is like having so many plutonium mines, whereas gathering the spent fuel into a limited number of reprocessing plants and storing the plutonium product simplifies and orders international control. The counterargument, of course, is that unseparated plutonium is much more inaccessible to would-be diverters. Although much of this is a matter of conjecture, the argument does raise three important points of principle.

1. Regardless of how the materials in question are stored, if they are to be under effective international control, the materials must be released either for processing or for use in research and development *only if the avowed purpose is clearly defensible*. Here again we see the dilemma of the fuel-supply-guarantee mechanism: What sort of international decision-making mech-

anism is to determine whether to respond favorably to requests that the material be released?

2. While the material is in storage, some means of international control must be maintained so that the material is not diverted for unauthorized purposes. The problem is that of international safeguards as well as physical protection.

3. Regardless of whether the mode of storage is national or international, the material must be physically on the soil of some sovereign state (unless extraterritorial arrangements can be worked out), and the state may decide to seize the material in open defiance of the covenant. Should such a bizarre move be made — or, for that matter, should *any* violation occur — the "international community" must be prepared to act. At the least, it must somehow distinguish the "safe" countries from the "unsafe" and locate the stores only in the safe countries. The difficulty is further compounded by the likelihood that because safety is at issue, the law of the land will require that sole proprietary rights in the materials be invested in the home government.

Modes of Fabricating Plutonium Fuel

The current technology of spent-fuel reprocessing is based on complete separation of the residual uranium, the newly created plutonium, and the highly radioactive waste. In fact, when fuel for the fast breeder reactor is fabricated, a mixture that is 80 percent plutonium and 20 percent uranium is created. It makes more economic sense, then, not to separate the two completely, but to extract them as a proper mixture. Technically, this choice is possible, and if fuel is fabricated in such a fashion, those who want to make nuclear explosives will have to go through the additional step of separation. This has come to be known as *coprocessing*. As a technical concept it is not new, and research and development on it have been conducted for some time. When employed in light-water reactors, plutonium-bearing fuel fabricated in this fashion presents additional technical problems. Whether or not coprocessing constitutes a good nonproliferation measure *per se* is somewhat questionable, for the following reasons:

1. Coprocessing presupposes the existence of a reprocessing plant and a plutonium-fuel fabrication plant (preferably in the

same location, for reasons of economics and physical protection) in "qualified" countries, from which the fabricated plutonium fuel will be shipped to the "unqualified" countries, i.e., those not granted access to the reprocessing technology. Here again is the familiar structure of dual values in the international nonproliferation structure.

2. Once the plutonium has been fabricated into fuel, and thus removed from radioactive waste, it can be separated fairly easily from the uranium in the fresh fuel. The major difficulty of spent-fuel reprocessing is the high radiation level of spent fuel; once that difficulty is removed, the problem becomes straightforward chemical engineering. The contribution that coprocessing can make toward nonproliferation is to extend the critical time required to fabricate nuclear explosives. In thus accepting the hardships attendant upon this fabrication mode, the "qualified" countries may simply be offering a good faith gesture, since the fuel will in any event be shipped out to the "unqualified" countries fabricated in the form of mixed oxide. This extension of critical time is nonetheless an important consideration; in the same sense, the willingness of the nuclear weapon states to accept international safeguards on their own peaceful fuel cycle is an important gesture.

3. It has also been proposed that some of the radioactive waste remain with the plutonium and uranium, or that fabricated plutonium fuel be preirradiated, so as to render the fuel further inaccessible. On nonproliferation grounds, this scheme (known as CIVEX) is obviously more desirable. At the same time, the costs of fabricating, transporting, and handling radioactive fuel would be enormous, and the problems of maintaining quality control, inspecting fuel, and assuring safe operation would be even more staggering. It is doubtful whether CIVEX can be looked upon as anything more than an interesting idea.

In any event, coprocessing or its radioactive variant is basically a means of extending lead time (which has come to be known in the trade as "conversion time"), namely, the time needed to take the fuel material in question, extract plutonium from it, and convert the plutonium into an explosive device. Different costs are associated with different schemes, some methods may be realistic and feasible, others not. But simply making weapons production difficult does not make it impossible.

Alternative Fuel Cycles

Over the years many cycles, each of a different degree of proliferation resistance, have been proposed. Many of them are technically interesting; most of them are industrially unpromising. But even the promising fuel cycles could not always be given their head. For example, the high temperature gas-cooled reactor has never succeeded in capturing the world's reactor market in spite of the fact that it is conceptually superior to the light-water reactor. For one thing, developing the technology of materials behavior in the high temperature helium environment has proved to be far more difficult than had originally been estimated. For another, it seemed foolhardy to invest time, money, and talent simultaneously in the development and maintenance of two complete sets of nuclear industries, namely, one for light-water reactors, the other for high temperature gas-cooled reactors. This was the case not only in the United States but also in a country like the United Kingdom, which invested heavily in the gas-cooled reactors over many years, but had to abandon the effort to raise gas temperature further. Throughout the history of nuclear power there have been many good reactor or fuel-cycle concepts that might have taken on the role played by the light-water reactor today. But history cannot be undone; we cannot make over the world's nuclear industry into another image, especially when economic incentives are so patently lacking.

The use of thorium as an alternative nuclear fuel, whether in high temperature gas-cooled reactors or otherwise, has often been discussed. When converted into uranium-233 in a reactor and separated through reprocessing, thorium can act as breeding fuel. The advantage of thorium fuel is that when breeder fuel is fabricated as a mixture of uranium-233 and uranium-238, the two are not easily separable. Extracting the uranium-233, which is excellent weapons-usable material, requires isotope-separation technology rather than chemical separation, and the former is technically more difficult than the latter. Critical time—for a bomb—becomes very long. Notwithstanding, and ignoring for the moment the fact that starting over with the thorium-based fuel cycle is unrealistic at this point, the basic issues are no different from those attending plutonium coprocessing. For example, a qualified country must undertake to reprocess thorium and fabricate thorium fuel. For an industrial plant that can perform uranium enrichment, separating uranium-233 is easy, because it employs the same technology. The use of thorium fuel, therefore, offers a means of buying longer access time, in the same qualified and un- qualified structure, but at a prohibitive price.

7
The Basic Structure
of Nonproliferation

Three considerations are evidently basic to the issue of non-proliferation:

1. Unless one assumes the unlikely event of a widespread consensus that there are sufficient uranium reserves, worldwide, to make the fast breeder unnecessary, the best that can be achieved is to delay the general spread of the sensitive plutonium and enrichment technologies and to prolong the critical time for components of peaceful nuclear power to be converted into nuclear explosives. Because sovereign states will always insist on their policy options, it would be irrational to expect them to take an irrevocable position on an issue—of fateful importance—that can be proved or disproved only after the fact. If we must wait for such universal consensus before undertaking to work out a program of nonproliferation, we are doomed from the start. We are not compelled to base such a program on any particular set of value judgments.

2. Any scheme that will delay the spread of sensitive technologies of uranium enrichment and spent-fuel reprocessing (plutonium extraction) implies a dichotomy between the "qualified" or "safe" countries and the "unqualified" or "unsafe" countries, the former maintaining and protecting the technology and production capacities and offering their services and supply guarantees to the latter. No matter how difficult politically it may be to present this fact to the world at large, it is not otherwise possible to devise viable schemes. We have no choice but to confront the difficulty head on. Weapons possession need not be where the lines are drawn, as between qualified and unqualified; more natural (and more palatable) is to draw them on the basis of

extant, large-scale industry—those lines are clear.

3. Different schemes to extend the critical time carry different price tags. If the price of a given scheme is so high that it defeats the nuclear option itself, or poses an industrially impossible proposition, then that scheme won't do. If, however, a proposal is within the realm of reality, politically, economically, and technically, then it is worth pursuing. On these terms, none of the proposals made to date are completely sound.

If these are indeed the three basic considerations in planning a nonproliferation program, then I need take up only three more matters. One is the role of international safeguards—one of the most misunderstood concepts in the nonproliferation pantheon. For a while, safeguards were considered foolproof, but once people perceived that they were not, many lost trust in them altogether. Properly, however, safeguards have never been conceived to be either foolproof or worthless. Combined with other measures, they are integral to any approach toward the goal of nonproliferation. The International Atomic Energy Agency and several of its member states once claimed that nuclear material accountancy is the only measure in the implementation of safeguards. Reliance on accountancy may have been an inevitable stage in the development of international safeguards, but it has created an impression that safeguarding is simply a *technology*, nothing more than the mechanical detection of diversion, in sufficient time to make actual proliferation impossible. But as we have seen, safeguards are part of a larger deterrent system, embracing (for example) political and economic assurances and sanctions, and as such should be selectively applied to countries with *and* without full fuel-cycle facilities.

In our previous discussion, we have distinguished "qualified countries" and "unqualified countries." *Qualified* countries are those for whom the cost of meaningful nuclear armament is very high, and for whom the price—political or otherwise—of violating the nonproliferation pledge is also very high. Countries already in possession of nuclear explosives do not automatically qualify; in that regard, we need consider only the cases of China and India. States for whom qualification *is* essentially automatic are those with advanced industrial technology, sufficient to maintain a nuclear power industry on at least the minimum viable scale. Since the nuclear fuel-cycle facilities that employ the more sensitive technologies will be located in these states, international safeguards do not necessarily need to be directed toward detecting the diversion of a single explosive device worth of nuclear material. What is required is that a credible system of control be established, so that nuclear facilities—whether those engaged in research, those under international control, or the national fuel cycle itself—are not operated in some unusual manner perhaps indicating that weapons-oriented activities are under way. To supplement these measures, surveillance over facilities of lesser proliferation risk, such as reactor plants and fabrication plants for low enriched fuel, should be carried on in such a manner as to detect major anomalies in the fuel-cycle system. More detailed technical proposals to implement this concept have been offered for international discussion.

For other countries, the cost and the price of violating the nonproliferation agreements are low. For these *unqualified* countries, the cost is low because the manufacture of even a single explosive device can have significant military, prestige, or political value. Here, safeguards will have to be sensitive to the diversion of a single device's worth of nuclear material. Since the international agreements would prevent the transfer of sensitive technologies to these regions and would provide for the shipment of plutonium and related materials only in a form of having a long access time, the detection of diversions at nuclear power plants and other facilities would be far less difficult than many have argued. But if any safeguard system is to be effective, it must be accompanied by international agreements that would follow up violations with appropriate sanctions. Assuring the potential violators of the certainty of sanctions is equivalent to raising the political ante before the fact.

The second matter that seems important to me at this point is the "international system" itself. People often talk about pre-arranged sanctions against violators of the nonproliferation pledge, but the history of sanctions—at least those established as international institutions—offers little support for their effectiveness. Because formal, multilateral institutions in the international arena inevitably operate under severe constraints, their effectiveness is sharply curtailed. Much the same must be said about such nonproliferation schemes as fuel-supply guarantee mechanisms and international plutonium-storage facilities, as we have seen. If formal, multilateral agreements must always precede the effective establishment of such an international system, simply obtaining consensus on how to proceed is likely to be an impossible task. All of the current discussion of nonproliferation, either within or outside the International Fuel Cycle Evaluation (INFCE) framework, along with all the good and sensible proposals to realize our mutual objectives, may end up being just so many good ideas. Reaching international accords on the schemes set forth here will be particularly difficult, since the schemes entail the concept of discrimination in many cases, albeit along the natural lines of demarcation in the industrial reality. It is very important that along with the efforts to obtain consensus in the multilateral and primarily technical forums concerning nonproliferation procedures, there should be simultaneous negotiations and discussions within a much more limited circle of technically advanced countries with common interests and a common view, wherein these countries might work out their own differences first—and, second, devise an optimal system of international mechanisms which might have some prospect for more universal acceptance.

Finally, these observations might be set against the provisions of the Nonproliferation Treaty. This is not the place to undertake discussion of Article VI, namely, the obligation of the nuclear weapons states to carry out nuclear disarmament (though its relevance to present purposes is obvious), but Articles I to III prompt comment. Although the current nonproliferation debate concerns itself chiefly with the obligations of the nonweapons states, and the concomitant means of verification (i.e., Articles II and III), if a weapon state violates Article I and covertly transfers either nuclear weapons or weapons-grade material, the credibility of the entire system will collapse instantly. It is vital that there be credible verification that this is not now happening, and credible assurances that it *will not* happen. Similarly, the fuel-supply guarantee is crucial to sustaining the division between qualified and unqualified countries, as are the assurances that sensitive technologies will not be transferred between the two. Violating the solemn pledge of supply guarantee, except where the guaranteed has committed actual acts of proliferation, would be as grave a sin as violating the nonproliferation pledge itself.

Nowhere in this work have I mentioned the future of the NPT. Whether a reasonable scheme of nonproliferation measures can be achieved within the existing framwork of the treaty, under the altered circumstances, may be debatable. What *is* clear is that the international community cannot tolerate the imposition of unilateral shifts in what is basically a multilateral accord. An attempt to update the NPT, if handled in a careless manner, can help to further erode worldwide confidence in this extremely important instrument of nuclear nonproliferation.

8
Comments on Mr. Imai's Position

Henry S. Rowen

Although Imai and I are in agreement on many factual matters and on a fair range of policy issues, I wish to focus here on several points of difference.

1. *Forgoing the use of plutonium poses a greater threat to security than the possibility that someone may build crude nuclear weapons ten to fifteen years from now.* This proposition asserts the essentiality of plutonium in the production of nuclear electric power. Yet nowhere does Mr. Imai claim that the use of plutonium is necessary or even economic in the current generation of light- and heavy-water reactors. Instead, he argues that the plutonium option needs to be created and the plutonium breeder adopted—but not before the year 2000. It is, then, a long-term need, but no less vital for that fact. ("The debate whether the uranium supply will last until 1995 or until 2010 is meaningless in any responsible plan.") If creating the plutonium option meant only doing research and development on this technology, as part of a balanced effort in which research and development is pursued across a wide variety of technologies, there would be no disagreement. I do not oppose conducting research on the plutonium breeder—in spite of its dangers—but I fail to see the basis for Imai's confidence about its importance in the twenty-first century, nor do I see the need to commit *now* to plutonium. How can Imai possibly know that among the array of technologies that will be available in the year 2000 and beyond, the plutonium breeder will be essential? In fact, the record of technological and resource forecasts does not generate much confidence in long-term predictions. With changes in relative prices and, more important, the

77

emergence of new technologies, prognostication on these matters should be made with great diffidence. The Japanese record of prediction may be good; the American record is not. For example, in 1891 the U.S. Geological Survey estimated that there was no oil in Texas, and in 1914 the Bureau of Mines estimated total future U.S. production at 6 million barrels. A 1962 consensus of U.S. oil companies' forecasts for oil production by 1980 was exceeded in 1972. From 1972 to 1977, official estimates of installed U.S. nuclear power fell by a factor of three. In 1970, the U.S. Cabinet Committee on Oil Import Control concluded that the world oil market would be more competitive in the future, and that organizing a cartel would become increasingly difficult. So much for forecasting—a difficult line of work.

It has been dogma in the nuclear industry since the beginning of the nuclear era that uranium is in such short supply that the world must sooner rather than later generate electricity from breeder reactors. The conviction has not been shaken—though it should have been—by announcements of unexpectedly large discoveries of uranium in the world since then, and discoveries continue to be made while the growth of installed nuclear power lags. Indeed, Imai makes the point that no one can say with conviction that nuclear power can meet the energy requirements of the future, and that pessimism is warranted for all of the energy candidates. In my view, at least skepticism is warranted.

His argument, however, rests less on the assumption that uranium will run out than it does on the concept of "energy independence." There are really two different objectives involved in that concept: one is security of supply; the other is energy autarky, or the production of most of one's energy at home. Security of supply is an objective that cannot be regarded lightly, given the 1973 experience of the industrialized countries with oil and the evident importance that governments attach to having secure supplies of fuel. But at the same time, dependence on fossil fuels will remain high even in economies that shift heavily toward nuclear electrification, and a significant degree of insulation from external forces can be gained at relatively low cost by having several years' supply of nuclear fuel on hand. In contrast, a policy of energy autarky is hardly a reasonable objective; it would be costly for the United States, and much more so for Japan.

Most important, given all of the uncertainties described by Imai, why should societies gamble on a commitment to a single technology for the distant future? This observation bears on the criticism of those who supposedly favor nonproliferation measures "at any cost." Trying to prevent proliferation "at any cost" might mean, as Imai suggests, giving up nuclear power. But avoiding the use of plutonium in the light- and heavy-water fuel cycles may save money. The costs of forgoing the plutonium breeder option are unknown and could be large, but I have not advocated it here, nor is it advocated by those who favor avoiding premature commitment to dangerous technologies. Are those who believe passionately in the essentiality of nuclear power really maximizing the likelihood of its continued development by resisting efforts to reduce its dangers?

If the importance of plutonium as a fuel is argued more vehemently than is warranted, so too is the *un*importance of so-called crude nuclear explosives. On that point, Imai seems too complacent. Even with reactor-grade plutonium, *reliable* yields in the kiloton range can be achieved. As a threat to urban targets, or even many military ones, such yields are by no means insignificant. (Note that the destructive area caused by blast varies not with yield but with the two-thirds power of yield. Moreover, the erratic operating history of many power reactors demonstrates that the plutonium in some of the spent fuel rods is more nearly "weapons grade" than "reactor grade" in character.)

The effect of such crude weapons may be more than psychological (a serious enough prospect in itself); today, deliverable nuclear weapons can be made by those whose technical competency is at less than the Nobel-laureate level. Imai's observation that only the truly desperate nation would use these weapons is not particularly comforting, given the frequency with which one group of people and then another do feel desperate; there may be those who would perceive, rightly or wrongly, some net advantage from their use. Confidence that weapons would be seen only as enhancing status and symbolically challenging the world order implies rather more trust in the stability of relations among states and within countries, especially in the less developed world, than seems warranted. In particular, it gives too little weight to actions that might be undertaken in the heat of war. It is this prospect that makes the wide availability of nuclear explosive materials so dangerous. What prudence might exclude in peacetime, passion might embrace in the heat of conflict.

2. *Because there are several alternative routes leading to nuclear explosives, concern about power-reactor plutonium is exaggerated; if a country is willing to pay the price, there is no effective way to stop it from getting bombs.* This amounts to saying that because one can be killed in any of several different ways, there is no point in trying to prevent any of them. But this is not what is proposed. I agree with Imai that *all* of the paths leading to a bomb should be included in a rational nonproliferation regime. In my text, I argue for the need to limit access to all nuclear explosive materials—the fissile material from large research reactors, criticality experiments, and enrichment facilities, as well as the plutonium from power reactors. The issue is impeding not only the optimum path toward a bomb but all possibly feasible paths that might be available to a government. Even governments that might feel little incentive to choose the technically optimum path—especially if doing so were to violate international agreements and invite sanctions—might not be deterred in a crisis or war from choosing a nonoptimum but feasible path. This is why the critical time to a bomb from a legitimate, safeguarded state must be made as long as possible. Imai's argument that there is no way to stop a determined government is too unqualified a proposition in the sense that it misses another key point. For several countries now, and no doubt for many in the future, the choice will not be a simple dichotomy: forgoing the bomb versus going for the bomb at any cost. Rather, the choice will be incremental, and it will be influenced by many factors, including the reactions to be expected from other countries.

Imai also tells us that we should worry more about the spread of advanced delivery technologies, and I agree that there is much to worry about in this regard. But, at a minimum, nuclear weapons can be delivered by commercial jet aircraft, which are capable of carrying thousands of pounds over thousands of miles. Limiting access to these aircraft is a losing proposition. Gaining access to fissile material remains the most difficult step on the critical path to deliverable bombs.

3. *Preventing technologies of major importance from pro-*

liferating is a political problem, not a technical one. Making this dichotomy is tempting, but inappropriate. Technology and politics — and economics, as well — interact too strongly. The technical paths that a government chooses will be influenced, to be sure, by the political costs incurred. If these costs are negligible, then a given technology will be sought. But if opting for a given technology — plutonium production reactors, reprocessing plants, enrichment plants — means incurring large political costs, then such choices might be avoided. And the magnitude of these political costs depends in part on international technological agreements in effect at the time choices are made.

4. *Restrictions on technology not only violate Article IV of the Nonproliferation Treaty but will fail in a world in which several suppliers are competing.* Imai's devotion to Article IV does not, apparently, extend to the less developed countries; it is important to delay, through export restrictions, the day when these countries acquire dangerous technologies. I do not see how he can have it both ways. The NPT is intended to have universal applicability, and Article IV contains no clause affording unrestricted technology transfer only to the countries of the "North." Unconstrained conformity to Article IV could, of course, bring many countries to the point of being days away from having deliverable nuclear explosives (though arguably this would infringe on Articles I and II). This prospect evidently makes Imai nervous as he contemplates the less developed countries, but not nervous enough to qualify his endorsement of Article IV.

In short, the view that embargoes on technology cannot work where there are competing suppliers seems inconsistent with advocating restrictions on technology transfer to the less developed countries. Moreover, it implies an absence, now and forever, of a common interest among governments. This gloomy view may be unwarranted, given the growing awareness of danger. Moreover, as Imai suggests, there can be value merely in slowing the rate of transfer.

5. *The advanced industrial countries should adopt an explicit policy of discrimination toward the less developed countries, and the nuclear fuel cycle should be organized internationally, with a limited number of technology centers.* This is a difficult subject, and my own treatment of it does not offer a solution. I agree with

Imai's objective, but I question its feasibility. For example, he rejects the distinction, central to the NPT, between weapon states and nonweapon states as the basis for a world system of control of dangerous technologies. His reasons are understandable; Japan has great industrial strength but is not likely to become a weapon state in the foreseeable future. Between the industrial powers and the less developed countries, there exists a large gap in technical capacity, in economically plausible roles for nuclear power, and in political stability. This distinction has been central to the functions, kept private for some time, of the *Suppliers Club*. Limiting to the industrialized countries those nuclear technologies that are especially crucial to the making of explosives is worth trying. This implies, among other things, an end to the distribution of research reactors, especially large ones, to nations around the world, and it provides a basis for closer nuclear cooperation among the industrialized states—between, for example, Japan and the United States. But attempting to draw an *explicit* line between North and South goes too far. Imai argues that limiting such technology centers to nuclear weapon states would violate the Nonproliferation Treaty. But, by the same token, political pressures to limit such centers to already industrialized states, and thus to exclude them from states that aspire to industrialization, might also be regarded as a violation. Instead, we need to pay a good deal more attention to promoting those universal rules that seem both useful and worth the cost.

6. *The United States behaves as if God has made a special arrangement for its nuclear weapons to be used only for beneficial purposes; this has not been universally accepted.* There is no reason why it should be. The question that seems to me most important here is not a moral one but a utilitarian one: does it help for the great powers to pledge themselves to nuclear disarmament (as they did in Article VI of the NPT)? Is such an eventuality within the realm of practical possibility? And what would its consequences be? In reality, the incentives some governments feel today to move toward nuclear weapons seem to be virtually independent of the size of the nuclear stockpiles of the great powers. Moreover, agitation for disarmament mainly affects the U.S. willingness to compete with the Soviet Union in this domain; if the United States were to undertake to make large, unilateral cuts (beyond the

substantial cuts it has already made in several important areas), there would be great unhappiness in Europe and Japan and intensified pressures in a number of countries to acquire their own nuclear weapons. Moreover, it is by no means clear that if by some magical means we achieved a world wholly freed of nuclear weapons, such a situation would persist. As Imai says, "to remove nuclear-weapons potential from the world is not possible."

7. *Perception of nuclear power as a means to fill the energy demand-and-supply gap during the rest of the twentieth century is also in a state of flux.* This is certainly true; the energy uncertainties that Imai discusses do indeed exist. But now, six years after the oil crisis of 1973 and the great increase in the price of oil and other energy resources, some clarity is also emerging. Take, for example, the demand for energy. It has grown very much less worldwide since 1973 than before, and less, too, in proportion to growth in economic output. There are good reasons for believing that this slow growth in demand will continue (unless OPEC collapses altogether and the oil price falls sharply; even then, governments would very likely impose restrictions on imports in order to keep dependence on imported oil from growing sharply). This implies slower growth in demand for electric power generally, and for nuclear electric power, than had been previously forecast, even though this growth will continue to be greater than for energy as a whole. The result will be less drain on uranium reserves, less pressure on uranium-enrichment capacity, less demand for spent-fuel storage-pond capacity, and less demand on other fuel-cycle activities than earlier estimates have anticipated.

This reduced drain on energy resources affords more time to develop alternatives to today's fuels — or alternatives to the breeders if it turns out to be too costly or too dangerous. This prospect does not, of course, mean that we relax efforts to assure security of supply for fuels. Nonetheless, the slowed growth in energy demand and therefore in installed nuclear capacity in many countries bears directly on the question of the adequacy of uranium supply. If installed nuclear capacity in the non-Communist world is around 600 gigawatts electric (GW_e) in the year 2000, that will constitute a sixfold increase over today's capacity. Even with possible improvements in the fuel efficiency of light-water reactors and heavy-water reactors, and less U-235 left in enrichment-plant tails, there will have to be a substantial increase in uranium output. But whatever the increase proves to be, it appears that it will be much less than was predicted only a few years ago.

Given these changes in the world of energy, we need to reassess some of the long-held beliefs about optimum strategies for nuclear fuel use.

Part 2
An American View

Henry S. Rowen

Introduction to Part 2

The U.S. government has been stirring up controversy in recent years by revising plans for its domestic nuclear power system, altering its nuclear export policies, and proposing similar changes worldwide. After an intensive internal review and a certain amount of debate against Jimmy Carter during his election campaign, President Ford announced in October 1976 that the United States was no longer committed to the commercial use of plutonium as a nuclear fuel.[1] The substance of the announcement was that certain components of the programmed fuel cycle were technically unnecessary, economically dubious, and dangerous. The statement focused attention on the dangers inherent in the wide distribution of nuclear explosive material that would result from current nuclear programs. President Carter not only endorsed the Ford administration's shift but went on to oppose early commitment by the United States to the plutonium breeder reactor.[2]

These moves against the use of plutonium have been widely criticized both at home and abroad. Indeed, ready acceptance of these moves would have been surprising given their challenge to certain beliefs that have become deeply embedded over more than thirty years—the belief that reactor-grade plutonium is not a nuclear explosive material, that the wide distribution of explosive materials is a necessary consequence of having nuclear technology, that it is too late to halt the spread of nuclear weapons because any nation wanting nuclear explosives can get them by one or another of several paths, and that the use of plutonium is needed to provide essential security of energy supplies.

The last of these propositions has emerged prominently in the opposition to the U.S. position. This counterargument, briefly, is that the United States, with its large supplies of fossil fuels, is able to eschew plutonium as fuel, but that other countries are less well endowed with energy resources, much more vulnerable to energy-supply interruption, and therefore much more in need of plutonium for fuel. Uranium is asserted to be so scarce, worldwide, as to require the early introduction of the plutonium breeder; or, in any case, most of the uranium is concentrated in so few countries that importers are not assured of supplies. Moreover, the Carter administration has developed its energy program on the assumption that oil and gas resources are being rapidly depleted and that there is likely to be a growing shortage of oil in the 1980s and thereafter. This view (together with observations about the United States being an "energy hog," depleting the world stock of fossil fuels) reinforces the concerns of those who reject the Carter administration's nuclear prescription. It is also said that, because the United States is an established nuclear weapons state, Americans do not share the perspective of people in other countries on the consequences of the wider distribution of nuclear explosive materials.

Further criticism includes the observation that the U.S. non-proliferation policy is having a perverse effect abroad, by increasing incentives to acquire the technologies useful for weapons programs. Moreover, the U.S. position, were it to be emulated by other nations, could increase the likelihood of war as nations scrambled for shrinking energy supplies.[3]

These counterarguments are advanced by many critics, including responsible officials in various governments who are in a position to influence policy. It is important to recognize, however, that perceptions of these matters have changed a great deal in the last few years not only in the United States but in a number of other countries, and that further changes are likely in the years ahead.

At this stage a major international exploration of these issues, the International Fuel Cycle Evaluation (INFCE), is under way. It is not clear what will come of current efforts to reconcile the objectives of developing the benefits of nuclear energy while seeking to limit the spread of nuclear explosives. At best, however, dangers will increase as the spread of nuclear technology inevitably brings more countries close to the ability to quickly acquire nuclear weapons. If reconciliation efforts fail, countries able to make nuclear explosives may do so—some might even use them. The increased prospect of catastrophe will intensify a popular revulsion against nuclear energy in all forms. In short, current efforts to obtain international cooperation in the development of nuclear energy can be viewed as an attempt to save nuclear energy not only from its critics but from its uncritical supporters.

The present situation is not stable. The United States has proposed a delay in commitment to some nuclear technologies that seem both especially dangerous and nonessential at the present stage of world energy development. Much remains to be done, however, in describing the characteristics of an international system that would permit the development of nucler energy while limiting its dangers. There is a need for principles on which a revised system might be based. The following discussion undertakes to describe these principles; it also makes evident some of the difficulties inherent in altering the existing system and making a new system work.

Notes

1. The principal decisions announced by President Ford on October 28, 1976, were included in the following statement: "I have decided that the United States should no longer regard reprocessing of used nuclear fuel to produce plutonium as a necessary and inevitable step in the nuclear fuel cycle, and that we should pursue reprocessing and recycling in the future only if they are found to be consistent with our international objectives." He also announced a number of implementing decisions, including domestic "deferral of the commercialization of chemical reprocessing of nuclear fuel"; called "upon all nations to join us in exercising maxiumum restraint in the transfer of reprocessing and enrichment technology . . . for a period of at least three years"; asserted that nuclear supplier nations—including the United States as a major supplier—have "a special obligation to assure that customer nations have an adequate supply of fuel for their nuclear power plants if those customer nations forgo the acquisition of reprocessing and uranium enrichment capabilities and accept effective proliferation controls." Ford called upon all nations to join in an international cooperative effort to develop a system of controls to prevent proliferation.

2. Carter's statement of April 7, 1977, announced among other things the indefinite deferral of the commercial recycling of plutonium, a restructuring of the U.S. breeder program deferring its date of commercialization, and a shifting of research and development to alternative nuclear fuel cycles.

3. For an example of this last assertion, see David J. Rose and Richard K. Lester, "Nuclear Power, Nuclear Weapons and International Stability," *Scientific American*, vol. 238, no. 4 (April 1978), pp. 45-47.

9
The Present International
System and Its Inadequacies

The present international rules for inhibiting the spread of nuclear weapons are largely those embodied in the Nonproliferation Treaty (NPT), in the International Atomic Energy Agency (IAEA) safeguards, in Euratom safeguards, and in bilateral agreements for cooperation among governments.

Components of the Present System

Nonnuclear weapons states adhering to the NPT agree not to receive or acquire nuclear explosives directly or indirectly (Article II); nuclear weapons states agree not to transfer, assist, encourage, or induce any nonnuclear weapons state to acquire nuclear explosives directly or indirectly (Article I), but they agree also to facilitate to the fullest the exchange of nuclear energy technology (Article IV), to carry out peaceful nuclear explosions for nonweapon states (Article V), and to reduce their own levels of nuclear armaments (Article VI).

The IAEA safeguards are intended to monitor the status of nuclear materials by confirming that they are handled in accordance with intergovernmental agreements. These agreements vary somewhat in scope, but in general they require the receiver of nuclear materials or technologies to guard them and to agree not to use them in explosives and not to transfer them to third parties.

The NPT has been widely interpreted as precluding any limitation on nuclear technology short of nuclear explosives (which are not defined technically in the treaty). Some nations, however, have adopted a more restrictive position than is implied by Article IV.

Canada ended nuclear cooperation with India in response to that country's use of plutonium from the Canadian-provided CIRUS reactor in its bomb test. The governments of France and Germany have said that they will no longer export reprocessing plants. The United States, despite a history of large-scale transfer of nuclear information and technology to other nations, has not exported the technologies of isotope separation or reprocessing and has sought to keep secret the most important isotope separation technologies. Now, under the Nuclear Nonproliferation Act of 1978, the United States will impose a more restrictive set of conditions on its nuclear exports. Under these conditions, all of the nuclear facilities of a country receiving U.S. exports must be under international safeguards and these countries cannot have exploded a nuclear device. Steps have also been taken to tighten the conditions under which highly enriched uranium (a nuclear explosive material) will be exported. The United States has also been engaged in the Nonproliferation Alternative Systems Assessment Program (NASAP), the purpose of which is to explore nuclear power generation technologies that incorporate the inhibiting of access to nuclear explosive material with the familiar criteria of low cost and nuclear safety.

Internationally, before INFCE was organized, several nuclear supplier nations adopted rules inhibiting the transfer of nuclear technologies. In 1974, the International Atomic Agency published an agreement among eight member nations indentifying a "trigger list" of materials and equipment that would not be exported unless covered by an IAEA safeguards agreement.[1] Subsequent talks among a group of supplier countries were also directed at inhibiting nuclear transfers.

Operationally, the most important parts of this system have been bilateral agreements between countries. These agreements vary over time and from one pair of countries to the next. Existing U.S. agreements vary a good deal, for example. Furthermore, agreements must now be brought into conformity with the 1978 Nonproliferation Act. For instance, the United States transferred heavy water to India for use in the famous CIRUS reactor in the 1950s without imposing limits on the use to which plutonium from that reactor might be put.[2] Most agreements currently in effect, however, provide the United States with approval rights over the reprocessing of spent fuel.

Although restrictions have been growing, it is important to recognize that the earlier interpretation of the rules meant virtually uninhibited transfer of technology; indeed Article IV of the NPT appears to call for such transfers. Articles I and II, however, imply that restraint should be applied well short of the transfer of nuclear explosives. The upshot in practice has been that the burden of preventing weapons acquisition has been placed almost entirely on the nonweapons states' pledge not to acquire explosives. The rule changes so far adopted have not altered this situation.

Inadequacies of the Present System

One of the most serious indictments of the present system is that nonsigners of the NPT, such as Spain and Brazil, have had no more difficulty in obtaining nuclear technology or fuel than have signers. The United States continues to supply India with nuclear fuels despite the fact that New Delhi has signed the NPT and despite India's explosive use of plutonium from an unsafeguarded reactor that used heavy water of U.S. origin—a clear violation of the spirit of the agreement between the two countries. The Canadian government found itself in a similar position regarding India but, unlike the United States, opted to terminate its cooperation with India.

Moreover, many of the agreements for cooperation on which these safeguards rest have turned out to be laxly drafted. For example, although most existing agreements give the United States a veto over the disposition of nuclear fuel of U.S. origin, agreements have not covered nuclear fuel from sources other than the United States when used in reactors of U.S. origin. In some cases the exporting country has lost important areas of control altogether; the United States has no direct control over nuclear fuel of U.S. origin made available directly to other countries through U.S. agreements with Euratom or with the IAEA.

Under the present rules, governments can come very close indeed to having bombs without violating existing safeguards.[3] It is not a violation of the NPT for a country to have possession of nuclear explosive materials.[4] Neither is it a violation to conduct experiments on the properties of conventional explosives or to investigate the rapid crushing of materials at very high pressures, i.e., to do research highly

relevant to developing the nonnuclear components of nuclear explosives. However, the Nuclear Non-Proliferation Act of 1978 pro-
hibits nuclear-related exports to countries that engage in activities
"involving source or special nuclear material and having direct significance for . . . nuclear explosive devices. . . ."[5] Even so,
the fact that plutonium from power reactors can reliably produce
explosions in the kilton range means that the increased number of
power reactors coming into operation will inevitably bring many
countries closer to the ability to make bombs. Other sources of explosive material include plutonium from research reactors (the
source used by India), highly enriched uranium used in research or
power reactors, and highly enriched uranium and plutonium used
in criticality experiments.[6]

By 1990, with the present programs and with the present international system, some thirty-five to forty nations could be in a
position to acquire nuclear explosives rapidly, whether or not any
of these govenments intend today to do so. The central problem is
not that there are many governments determined to go ahead. It is
evident that most governments that today have the necessary
technical and economic resources are not bent on getting nuclear
explosives — because they do not feel threatened, or because they
perceive that their security is better provided for by alliance ties, or
because they see even graver risks in acquiring these weapons than
in not having them. Nonetheless, the numerous entrenched
regional rivalries, the conflicts that are certain to occur, and the
growing capacity of countries to move quickly to acquire explosives, when taken together, are grounds for grave concern. Furthermore, many of the countries that will acquire greater competency
in nuclear technology in the next decade are outside of the major
alliance systems; some have intense regional rivalries or are
unstable. An incomplete list of rivalries includes the tension between the two Koreas, between Taiwan and China, Israel and the
Arabs, India and Pakistan, and South Africa and its neighbors.
Yugoslavia lies precariously between East and West. A mixture of
incentives might cause the governments of such countries as Iran,
Brazil, Argentina, and Spain to deliberately shorten the lead time
to nuclear explosives.

In many such relationships, the fear that a rival may be on the point of getting nuclear explosives provides a strong incentive to get nuclear explosives first—or at least "not to be second," as the Israelis put it. It is plausible that governments in a crisis or a war might find that supreme national interest dictates getting nuclear explosives as quickly as possible and even, in the passion of war, using them as the United States did in 1945.

Although to a considerable extent the existing agreements provide a "cover" under which many countries move closer to an acquisition capability, the existing safeguards have value. Despite the basic inconsistencies incorporated in the NPT during its negotiation, commitments not to acquire nuclear explosives have not (for the most part) been entered into lightly, nor are they likely to be abandoned readily. But the existing system has large defects.

The 1978 Nonproliferation Act is intended to plug the most obvious holes. When fully in force, nuclear cooperation will cease if a recipient country detonates a nuclear explosive or abrogates or materially violates IAEA safeguards or any guarantees it has given under agreements for cooperation; U.S. consent for transfer of materials or equipment to third parties is required; and no materials transferred or produced from U.S. equipment may be reprocessed without prior U.S. approval. All the bilateral and trilateral agreements for cooperation have to be revised to reflect these requirements, although the president is given authority to modify or delay specific implementation of the terms of the laws.

Clearly, there are sharp limits to what the United States or other suppliers of uranium or nuclear technology, such as Canada or France, can or should do unilaterally, or even in concert. What is needed is a general rethinking—and arguably revision—of the international system.

An Assumption of Substantial— but Bounded—Common Interest

It is sometimes observed that the diffusion of the capacity to make nuclear explosives presents no security problem to country X, that it is only a problem for the great powers, that it will hurt the Russians more than us, that if a government is determined to get a bomb it will do so, or that, in any case, there is nothing we Germans or Japanese or Americans can do that will affect things very much. These views imply an absence of a strong common interest in preventing wide access to nuclear explosives, or at least an incapacity to affect the process. The latter view, on examination, often amounts to an implicit assumption of only a weak common interest; some of those who say that nothing can be done are silent on the possible consequences of doing nothing.

A view at the other extreme would be that there is indeed an overriding universal interest in stopping the spread of nuclear weapons, and that the central problem is keeping explosives out of the hands of terrorists and blocking those officials in governments who, blind to the common good, would move with all deliberate speed to acquire bombs.

The revealed behavior of most governments has been somewhere in between. Clearly, there have been inhibitions against proceeding; most of the twenty-five or so governments able to have nuclear explosives today have elected not to acquire them. In the future, should more governments decide to get them, those inhibitions would erode rapidly. But even for those that do go ahead, some restraints are likely to remain. For example, if it is true, as widely reported, that Israel has nuclear weapons, it has nonetheless felt constrained from visibly deploying and testing them. This restraint can plausibly be attributed to a desire to avert damaging Arab and Western responses. Similar restraints, together with domestic opposition, exist in many countries.

In short, even though there appears to be a common interest in avoiding the obvious steps that would spread nuclear explosives, the close connection between civilian and military uses of nuclear energy has not been perceived clearly enough even within governments that have no obvious intent to acquire weapons. For its part, the United States has been, at best, inconsistent in its concerns over the military applications of the nuclear transfers it has made. The U.S. view has now changed greatly. This pattern is true of a growing number of countries—France, for instance. But common interest can be in conflict with a particular interest, for instance a reactor sale that needs to be "sweetened" with enrichment or reprocessing technology.

In general these particular interests will not be unbounded.

Hence, the task is to find those courses of action that could be effective and have a tolerable cost, and try to win wide acceptance for them internationally, within a revised system.

The Concepts of "Critical Time" and "Legal Starting Point"

The prospect of a world in which many governments are within days of possessing explosives without having violated the existing rules has revived a concept implicit in some of the first proposals set forth at the end of World War II for limiting the dangers of nuclear power, but a concept that has not been pursued systematically until recently. This is to focus on the "critical time" required to move from a "safeguarded" state to the possession of explosives. Lengthening that time has several benefits: it allows an increased period in which to detect moves toward a bomb, and hence lengthens the time in which a response can be mounted by other states. This could have a discouraging effect. Furthermore, the longer this time can be made, the less costly the counter measures need to be, because the moves to make a bomb are detected at an earlier stage. A long critical time should also make it easier for any government *not* interested in possessing nuclear explosives to demonstrate that it does not have them, nor is it close to having them.

The concept of critical time should not be viewed solely in the context of the relationship between a supplier of nuclear materials and recipients. However important this relationship, it is likely to be overshadowed by relationships within regions and by ties between regional powers and great ones. The concerns of the governments of, say, Korea, Taiwan, or Iran are likely to be dominated by the possibility of war with neighbors and the prospects of support from large allies and supporters. Viewed in this light, even a government with a secure supply of nuclear fuel might nevertheless hold back from overtly acquiring nuclear weapons for fear of triggering unwanted reactions from regional neighbors or great powers. Such concerns might even produce decisions not to take final steps to acquire weapons.

A little reflection will suggest that a lot is implied in the definition of critical time. For one thing, it implies both a starting position and an end position. Today, as noted earlier, the legal starting point can be the possession of nuclear explosive materials and expertise in nonnuclear technologies useful in making atomic weapons. (Here, the word "legal" simply means in violation neither of existing bilateral agreements for cooperation nor of the NPT.) Nuclear explosive materials might be legally available today from several sources (although in some cases not without approval from the United States under the provisions of the Nonproliferation Act):

1. As highly enriched material at the "front end" (i.e., as fuel) for research reactors or high temperature gas reactors
2. Through isotope separation of U-235 from natural uranium or from low enriched uranium received as reactor fuel
3. Through the use of plutonium acquired from spent fuel from large research or electric power reactors. The plutonium might be extracted through use of reprocessing plants at home or on contract with nations (e.g., Britain or France) that sell reprocessing services, or from possible future "multinational" reprocessing plants. Another source is plutonium transferred from other nations for criticality experiments or breeder research and development.

This list is not exhaustive, but it shows that there are today many legal paths to shortening the critical time.

What about the "end position?" This might be any of a large number of nuclear postures: the development of one or a few weapons to have in a crisis or to use in a war; or the possession of a few (e.g., three) or more than a few (e.g., twenty to fifty) assembled or nearly assembled kiloton-yield weapons that might or might not have been tested. Alternatively, the end position might be not a *posture* but a *program*, one intended to progress from weapons of simple design to ones of more sophistication, not excluding thermonuclear weapons and the accumulation of a sizable weapons stockpile.[7]

It should be evident that, although the concept of critical time is central to an understanding of the processes that influence incentives for and against moves to acquire nuclear weapons, an "adequate" critical time is not the same in each situation. Later discussion will explore some of the complexities encountered in applying this concept.

Notes

1. This agreement, published in IAEA INFCIRC/209, was the product of the group known as the "Zanger Committee." It is described in "World Armaments and Disarmaments," *SIPRI Yearbook*, Stockholm International Peace Research Institute, 1977.

2. For an analysis of the subsequent wavering attempts of U.S. and Canadian authorities to block India from making a bomb using plutonium from CIRUS, see Roberta Wohlstetter, "'The Buddha Smiles': Absent-Minded Peaceful Aid and the Indian Bomb," *Pan Heuristics*, April 30, 1977.

3. A. Wohlstetter et al., "Moving Toward Life in a Nuclear Armed Crowd?" *Pan Heuristics*, April 1976. This report presented many of the concepts that became the basis for changes in civilian nuclear policies of the Ford administration. This report was followed in early 1977 by the publication of *Nuclear Power Issues and Choices*, Report of the Nuclear Energy Policy Study Group, (Cambridge, Mass: Ballinger). This report, supported by the Ford Foundation and administered by the MITRE Corporation, strengthened the case for avoiding the use of readily fissionable materials in commerce, including deferring commitment to the plutonium breeder. It was publicly endorsed by President Carter in support of his nuclear policy.

4. The NPT speaks of "devices," not nuclear explosive "materials" such as plutonium or highly enriched uranium.

5. See Section 307 of the Nuclear Non-Proliferation Act of 1978.

6. For many years, until recently, an unnecessary and unwarranted degree of ambiguity was allowed to persist on the usability of high burn-up (so-called reactor-grade) plutonium in explosives. The effect of high burn-up is to increase the proportion of isotopes of plutonium higher than Pu-239, especially the nonfissile isotope Pu-240. This lowers the expected yield and increases its variance. Yet, from the period of the Manhattan Project on, it has been known that explosives in the kiloton range could be reliably achieved with such material.

7. In each of these cases, essential system components would include delivery vehicles, warning, active and passive defenses of delivery systems, and, not least, command and control systems.

10
Four Principles for
a Safer International System

The inadequacies of the present system lead to a consideration of changes in this system that might meet the dual criteria of making civilian nuclear energy less susceptible to being turned to weapons purposes while at the same time enabling nuclear energy for civilian uses to develop. No one approach will suffice; a strategy with several components is needed.

One: Direct Moves Toward Safer Technologies

Under this principle three types of actions are needed.

Agreeing to Limit Dangerous Technologies. In brief, states that are not nuclear weapons states and do not wish to be so regarded by others (nonnuclear weapons states in the terminology of the NPT) should not possess sizable quantities of readily fissionable material, materials quickly convertible to explosives, or the technology for rapidly making sizable amounts of explosive materials.

This principle focuses on the most difficult task in getting nuclear explosives, that of acquiring readily fissionable materials, including uranium-235, uranium-233, and plutonium. Materials "quickly convertible to explosives" include separated plutonium, highly enriched uranium for use in high temperature gas reactors, marine reactors, and large research reactors, and plutonium contained in fresh mixed oxide fuel (MOX). The technology for rapidly making sizable amounts of readily fissionable materials includes reprocessing plants and at least those enrichment technologies that could quickly be converted from producing low enriched nuclear fuel to highly enriched uranium.[1]

Over time, the effectiveness of the existing supplier constraints will gradually erode as technology adaptable to the manufacture of nuclear weapons spreads. Therefore, obtaining international agreement on limitations on dangerous technologies along these lines should be at the heart of a safer international system.

Restricting Transfer of Dangerous Technologies. Although voluntary adherence to a more or less common set of practices is necessary in the long run, it is important that limitations continue to be placed on the transfer of technologies that are especially useful for making bombs and that are, in general, not essential for economic uses of nuclear energy. Just as few would expect — or want — to see free commerce in nuclear weapons at any point in the future, so it should be with especially dangerous and economically dubious technologies. Even when many more nations have the technical and industrial capacity to make nuclear explosives, some will not, and maintaining barriers to further spread will be important indefinitely. Barriers will also be needed in order to impede access to advanced designs of weapons.

Expanding Research and Development on Safer Nuclear Technologies. In the past, criteria for choosing nuclear research and development projects have centered on lowering energy costs, increasing efficiency in the use of uranium, and improving reactor safety. Now, the need to heed critical time as a design criterion is more widely recognized and is being included among the relevant criteria for research on future nuclear systems.

Two: Strengthening Incentives to Adopt Safer Technologies

Three types of actions might help to increase the relative attractiveness of safer technologies.

Practicing Nondiscrimination in Commercial Activities. States accepting constraints on the development of the full range of possible nuclear technologies should not suffer discrimination in the commercial uses of nuclear energy. The corollary of this principle is that nuclear weapons states should not engage in commercal activities they would like to see denied the nonweapons states. This philosophy underlay the Ford and Carter administrations' decisions to forgo plutonium recycling at home. The principle implies the sharing of benefits from nuclear activities carried out in certain locations, e.g., fuel centers, with other states. At present there is little economic advantage (and on current evidence an economic disadvantage) from recycling in light-water reactors. The economic prospects of the plutonium breeder are uncertain at best. But even if there were an economic advantage in using especially dangerous technologies, prudent consideration might cause them to be avoided. But if, after all, dangerous technologies were adopted by the weapons states, any economic advantages derived should be shared with the nonweapons states.

Helping with the "Front End": Assuring Security of Fuel Supply at a Fair Price. Everyone wants to obtain energy, including nuclear fuel, as reliably and cheaply as possible. There is an important difference, however, between energy independence, which implies a policy of autarky, and security of supply, which implies confidence in having fuel available when needed. Much of the expressed interest in the use of plutonium fuel, especially in the plutonium breeder, derives from the desire for import security. Insecurity also provides an incentive for the development of national enrichment capabilities, even though, as in the case of the breeder, the contribution to security of energy supply would be modest, and there is a good deal of uncertainty about the economics of small enrichment plants. International steps seem to be needed to increase the general confidence that all nations adhering to the restrictions in the use of nuclear energy will have assured supplies of uranium and enrichment services over time.

Helping with the "Back End." The use of a "once-through" fuel cycle with storage of unreprocessed spent fuel is a system that promises to be viable for a long time.[2] But the accumulation of spent fuel poses a storage problem in some countries and presents a growing safeguard problem. International cooperation in the removal of spent fuel and in its safe storage should be an integral part of an amended international system.

Three: Reducing the Demand for Nuclear Explosives

Any international arrangement must address itself to the circumstances in which a government might perceive a compelling need to acquire nuclear weapons. Some governments may face an adversary capable of an overwhelming nonnuclear attack; some may face an adversary armed with nuclear weapons or one in a position to quickly get these weapons. Help with nonnuclear arms and alliance ties addresses these concerns, although such transfers and ties do not necessarily solve the problem (e.g., how reliable *are* the alliance ties, and even with added conventional arms, how safe would the nation be?). The principle of reducing the demand for nuclear explosives does not endorse unconstrained arms transfers, but it does recognize the legitimacy of such transfer where it can be argued that nonproliferation goals would thereby be advanced.

Four: Increasing the Expected Cost of Moving from a Legal State

Three types of measures might increase the burden of the development of nuclear weapons by a nonweapons state.

Increasing the Barriers to Making Weapons from Civilian Materials. Radioactivity in spent fuel is a natural barrier, one available without cost so long as the net residual fuel value is less than the cost of mining fresh uranium. It should be an objective of a nonproliferation regime to incorporate comparable barriers related to fresh fuel and the choice of technologies for providing enrichment services. The cost of providing such barriers should be incorporated in the choice of which energy technologies to develop and build.

Improving Safeguards. The measures listed above would reduce the extent to which the "noise" created by civilian activities obscures the "signals" of ominous military ones. But it is also important to increase the sensitivity of the apparatus for detecting "signals" of moves from a legal state toward weapons. This can be done through improving the IAEA safeguard system. Measures of interest include continuous monitoring of enrichment plants, to confirm that they are producing low enriched fuel, and of spent-fuel storage, to confirm that the fuel remains in place.

Applying Sanctions. For those countries that violate agreements, there should be costs. Ending nuclear cooperation might be useful, but a much wider range of economic and other sanctions might be undertaken. To repeat a point made above, the most important effective responses are likely to be those outside the arena of fuel supply.

Notes

1. The United States' choice of centrifuge technology for its next increment of enrichment undermines this principle. Centrifuge cascades can be converted from an output of 3 percent enriched product to an output of 90 percent enriched product more rapidly than can diffusion cascades.

2. "Once-through" refers to the current practice of removing spent fuel from reactors and storing it. This is in contrast with the proposed "recycle" system in which the spent fuel would be sent to a reprocessing plant in order to extract the plutonium and unburned uranium; the wastes from this process would then have to be stored.

11
The Benchmark Case

The present types of light- and heavy-water reactors, operated under safeguards, with no reprocessing of spent fuel and early removal of spent rods from the storage pond, provide a standard (or *benchmark*) to be used in evaluating how readily the proliferation of other technologies can be limited.[1] The low enriched or natural uranium fuel used by these reactors is not explosive material, nor is the spent fuel. These two technologies are capable of providing nuclear electric power beyond the end of the century, taking into account known and probable uranium supplies. Such a system, with incremental improvements, could operate at least for the next quarter century, and probably well beyond.

The spent fuel leaving reactors is highly radioactive, and even if away-from-reactor storage is used, spends several months in cooling ponds at reactor sites. With time, it becomes easier to handle and therefore to reprocess, although radiation levels, say, five years after removal from the reactor would still be intense. A system that would continue to provide a higher level of protection should include removal of spent fuel from the commercial reactor site after an initial cooling period and transfer to concentrated storage sites in safe locations.

Nonetheless, there is uncertainty as to how much protection is provided, with spent fuel, by the radiation barrier itself. According to one view, not much. A government might undertake to build covertly a small reprocessing plant and separate plutonium, and at the same time do the development work on the nonnuclear components of a bomb. Although there is uncertainty about the lead time as well as the probability of success of such an undertaking, it is important to note that if a government has agreed to forgo reprocessing, the construction of such a plant would be a violation of an international understanding; moreover, secrecy would not be assured.

There is one point that should not be overlooked. If it is true, as some argue, that the radiation barrier in the back end of the fuel cycle presents little obstacle to getting plutonium, or that new isotope separation technologies will make it easy to enrich uranium to a concentration usable in weapons, then the entire nuclear enterprise is in real trouble. In such a world, the possession of a nuclear reactor would be tantamount to having the ability to produce usable bomb material on short notice — a condition of doubtful political acceptability.

For the present it appears that "once-through" systems, which do not produce nuclear explosive materials, provide a useful standard against which to measure the weapons-proliferation resistance of alternative technologies. Such a standard or benchmark obviously only makes sense if international agreements for the use of nuclear power preclude other means of legitimately obtaining nuclear explosive materials, a point often overlooked in criticism of "once-through" systems.[2] Therefore, agreements covering isotope separation facilities, research reactors, criticality experiments, and other facilities are needed.

Because readily fissionable materials are present in both the fresh fuel used in nuclear reactors and in the spent fuel, it is difficult to see how to improve on the proliferation resistance represented by this benchmark system, other than to abandon nuclear power altogether. There are, however, other nuclear fuel cycles that may be able to offer a comparable barrier to the construction of bombs while at the same time being more economical in the consumption of uranium. Improved models of light-water reactors promise to achieve improvements in uranium burn-up close to that achievable through reprocessing — a saving of about 30 percent of total uranium requirements (compared to today's usage); and a further reduction to about 40 percent may be possible with greater "tails stripping" through the use of more economical isotope separation technology. In a steady-state nuclear system, the recycling of plutonium and uranium would replace about 35 percent of the uranium that would otherwise have to be mined. In a growing system the saving is less; for the United States, the recycling saving to the end of the century would be about 20 percent. If substantial uranium-conserving changes were to be introduced in light-water reactors by 1990 and partially retrofitted to existing plans, the uranium saving to 2000 could be comparable to that of reprocessing.

Today's heavy-water reactors are about 20 percent more economical in the use of uranium than today's light-water reactors operated without reprocessing the spent fuel, and that figure can be raised to 40 percent through the use of slightly enriched uranium.[3] The thorium-uranium-233 breeder "denatured" with uranium-238 might also meet the benchmark test of proliferation safety while saving greatly on uranium. Institutional arrangements would have to be adopted to take account of the fact that some of the uranium-238 added to "denature" the uranium-233 would be converted to plutonium. This fuel cycle would meet the test if breeding could be limited to international fuel centers, with only the denatured fuel shipped widely for use in burner reactors, and the spent fuel returned to waste management centers.[4] This fuel cycle, however, is not fully developed.

Other proposals have been made to achieve increases in the critical time in a system that recycles plutonium as fuel. One is the joint production (coprocessing) of uranium and plutonium in order to produce mixed oxide fuel (MOX) directly. However, unirradiated MOX does not offer much of a barrier to getting explosive materials; moreover, a plant operated in this way could probably be switched quickly to producing a pure plutonium stream.

The benchmark standard might be approximated by incorporating a radiation barrier in fresh fuel. This might be done by preirradiation of fresh fuel, by *spiking* it with fission products, or by leaving some fission products in the fuel during reprocessing. However, the suitability of incorporating fission products in thermal reactors is even more questionable than it would be in fast reactors. (Thermal reactors are more readily "poisoned" in their operation through the presence of fission products than are fast reactors.) Moreover, the application of this standard should take account of the preference that governments have for security of supply; one way they are expressing this preference is to have several years' supply of fresh fuel on hand. This implies that the radioactive level of the fresh fuel would have to be such as to provide a substantial barrier for at least several years. Moreover, the fresh fuel containing plutonium would require continued monitoring during this state just as would spent fuel if it remained accessible.

The most prominent of the spiking schemes is the CIVEX proposal developed by Chauncey Starr of the Electric Power Research Institute and Walter Marshall of the U.K. Atomic Energy Authority. In this scheme some fission products are left in the fresh fuel thus creating a radioactive barrier. The scheme is designed to work only with fast reactors, not thermal ones; therefore, it would not be applicable to the reactors that will dominate the nuclear industry for the next quarter-century and more. Moreover, the necessity to remove radioactivity will add an unknown amount to fuel fabrication costs. This barrier would doubtless help with the problem of terrorists seizing fresh fuel but as in the case of coprocessing discussed above, it is not clear yet how much of a barrier would be created for governments operating their own CIVEX reprocessing plants. And if governments have their reprocessing done elsewhere and receive CIVEX fuel from others, how have they helped their supply-security problem by adopting the breeder?

Notes

1. The on-line designs of heavy-water reactors places additional demands on the inspection system to assure the accountability of all fuel rods.

2. Chauncey Starr, "Nuclear Power and Weapon Proliferation — The Thin Link," presented at the American Power Conference, Chicago, April 19, 1977. Subsequently, Starr has endorsed the principle of changing the rules to preclude dangerous activities and has accepted the once-through light-water reactor and heavy-water reactor as the benchmark as a basis for appropriate design criteria for breeder fuel. See his "The Separation of Nuclear Power from Nuclear Proliferation" paper delivered at the Fifth Energy Technology Conference, Washington D.C., February 27, 1978.

3. C. E. Till and Y. I. Chang, "Uranium Resource Implications of Fuel

Cycle Selection on Proliferation Grounds," RMS-TM-12, Argonne National Laboratory, January 1, 1978.

4. Harold A. Feiveson and Theodore B. Taylor, "Security Implications of Alternative Fission Futures," *Bulletin of the Atomic Scientists*, vol. 32, no. 10 (December 1976) pp. 14-18.

12
Economic Analysis
of the Benchmark System

The costs of adhering to the benchmark system through at least the end of the century would be low, perhaps even negative. From the early days of the nuclear era, the main argument for recycling uranium and plutonium from spent fuel in light-water reactors and for introducing the plutonium breeder as soon as possible has been that uranium was thought to be scarce, and that efficiency in its use should therefore be maximized. This is an improper criterion; taken literally it would make nuclear power impossibly costly, as increasing amounts of capital were expended to save each pound of uranium.

There is no assurance that electric power with plutonium recycling would be less costly than electric power without it, and recent evidence supports earlier analyses that it might well cost more. At the time of President Ford's decision to defer a commitment to reprocessing, there were many assertions about the great savings, not only in uranium but also in dollars, from recycling. By now it is widely accepted inside as well as outside of the United States that recycling in light-water reactors is uneconomical at anything like the current uranium price.[1] The price that the French are reportedly proposing to charge the Germans and Japanese for reprocessing some of their spent fuel—around $500 per kilogram in 1978 dollars—has probably had a larger effect in changing attitudes at home and abroad than the U.S. estimates of reprocessing cost. By now, the argument for going ahead with reprocessing has shifted to the need to prepare for the introduction of the breeder.[2] More will be said here on this argument.

An important reason for plutonium's prospective unimportance

as a fuel over the next several decades is that the uranium supply
has turned out to be much more adequate relative to the demand
for it than has often been predicted. Large reserves of uranium
were discovered in the United States and in several other countries
during the 1950s and 1960s, with the result that the real price of
uranium fell by 60 percent from the early 1950s to the early 1970s.
Even at the much higher price of uranium that has prevailed since
1973, which has made the long-term contract price in real terms
roughly that of the early 1950s ($30 to $40-plus per pound of
uranium oxide, U_3O_8, in 1978 dollars), recycling in light-water
reactors is not attractive on fuel-economy grounds.

Estimates of uranium reserves in relation to projected demands
reinforce this conclusion. The U.S. Department of Energy (former-
ly the Energy Research and Development Administration — ERDA)
now estimates 4.3 million tons for the United States, including
speculative reserves, in its "forward cost" category of $50 a pound
or less (in 1977 dollars).[3] It is, of course, to be expected that the
size of proven reserves is very much smaller than that ultimately
producible at a given price. It does not pay a resource-producing
industry to spend money to develop reserves except in relation to
expected demand; in practice this often results in proven reserves
covering expected consumption for the next ten years or so. Current U.S. proven reserves will be adequate for much longer than
this, well into the 1990s. Moreover, there are good reasons for
believing that these resource estimates are biased downward. First,
no allowance is made of more than traces of uranium in Alaska,
which is largely unexplored. Second, there has been relatively little
exploration in the contiguous forty-eight states outside of the
western sandstones that have been a rich source of uranium;
uranium has been found elsewhere in the world in other types of
formations that also exist in the United States. Third, the
technology of uranium exploration and development will continue
to improve over time; a recent example is the use of *in situ* solution
methods. These technology advances will increase the resources
available at a given cost. Fourth, the amount of by-product
uranium produced along with other minerals in the years to come
has been underestimated.[4]

To be sure, not all the forces at work will necessarily act to hold
the price of uranium down. For example, recent changes in health

and safety laws have had the effect of increasing the cost of uranium. In any case, predicting the price of any mineral in the distant future is a hazardous matter. But there are no compelling reasons for expecting the price of uranium to increase in real terms in the next quarter-century, and there are reasons to expect the price to decline in real terms.[5]

Changes have also been taking place on the demand side. Estimates of uranium demand are derived from the estimates of installed nuclear plants capacity, and these projections have been shrinking year by year since 1970. In 1970, the U.S. AEC estimated that there would be 300 GW_e of nuclear power installed by the end of 1985; a recent estimate is about one-third as much, 103 GW_e.[6] Similar shrinkage has taken place in estimates for nuclear power in the year 2000. In 1974, ERDA's "middle" estimate for the year 2000 was 1,110-1,200 nuclear GW_e; in contrast, its 1977 projection was 380 GW_e. In a recent report, a range of installed nuclear capacity shown for the year 2000 was 148 GW_e to 380 GW_e, the first figure corresponding to the amount of nuclear capacity installed, under construction, or for which a construction license had been issued as of early 1978.[7] With only about 100 GW_e installed in 1985, reaching the upper end of this spread would mean adding capacity at the rate of 9 percent a year after 1985, a rate far above the expected growth in electricity demand. Attaining this level would mean a rapid expansion in reactor construction and new orders. But even at that level, the U.S. nuclear industry would consume only about 0.75 million tons of U_3O_8 between now and the year 2000 — assuming no improvement in uranium burn-up — an amount about equal to currently proven reserves.[8]

Similarly large reductions are taking place in forecasts of nuclear power outside of the United States. The IAEA in 1975 estimated the non-Communist nuclear capacity in 2000 at 2,005-2,480 GW_e; in 1977, the range was 1,000-1,890 GW_e. Even the low end of the new low projection is probably much too high. On present trends, the range of 500-800 GW_e seems most plausible.

A similar forecast can be made for enrichment services. Contrary to the belief widely held a few years ago, there will be no shortage of enrichment services in the foreseeable futue. World consumption of enrichment services in 1985 will be about 25 million separative work units (SWU) (at 0.2 percent tails), only 40 percent as much as widely estimated only a few years ago. The projected supply is over 40 million SWU. It is evident that there will be a large surplus of enrichment capacity, and that no additional capacity beyond that now programmed will be needed on-line until the 1990s.

The uranium supply-and-demand situation worldwide is likely to be even more favorable than that of the United States, largely because nuclear growth abroad is also proceeding more slowly than expected, thus reducing demand, while the increase in the supply of uranium is sure to be greater outside of the United States than inside, for with a few exceptions far less exploration for uranium has taken place elsewhere. An OECD/IAEA estimate (as of 1977) places the (non-Communist) world proven and reasonably assured reserve resources (from known deposits) at 5.6 million tons of U_3O_8.[9] This is well in excess of the estimated cumulative need for about 1.7 million tons through the year 2000, which is based on a high rate (8 percent a year) of installation of nuclear capacity outside of the United States beyond 1985, to a (non-Communist) world total for the year 2000 of about 800 GW_e.

More uranium will be needed after the year 2000 to fuel the reactors that will then be operating throughout their lifetimes and to support further additions to capacity. The evidence strongly supports the conclusion that uranium resources exist to support the nuclear industry well into the twenty-first century without dependence on the plutonium breeder. For example, if world[10] installed nuclear capacity in the year 2000 were 800 GW_e, and if it were then to triple in the next twenty-five years, reaching 2,400 GW_e by the year 2025 (a growth rate of 2.8 percent annually), the uranium consumed by that date and required through the lifetime of the reactors then installed would be comparable to a current lower bound estimate of the world's relatively low-cost uranium resources.[11]

Even if the uranium is in the ground, there remains the question of finding it, developing mines, and producing it on a schedule that meets the growth in installed capacity. Various impediments to a rapid growth in uranium production may exist, especially political impediments. But the intense search for uranium now taking place as a result of the price increase in the mid-1970s, together with the slowdown in projections of installed capacity, suggest that production-rate constraints will not be binding.

The future cost of uranium has an important bearing on the choice of future nuclear technologies. No one can say with confidence now what the costs of the alternative technologies will be in the first quarter of the twenty-first century. But the evidence supports the conclusion that there is not a compelling case for rushing ahead with a commitment now to building plutonium reprocessing plants and demonstration breeders. Moreover, there are reasons for postponing some dangerous activities until later in this period — the dangerous activities may never have to be carried out. Nonetheless, the timing would be a matter of some importance if there were strong grounds for believing that plutonium breeders might be economically competitive soon.

In order to understand why this is unlikely, it is important to grasp the fact that the sole advantage promised by the breeder is a reduction in uranium consumption. Only if uranium is quite costly would the breeder be cheaper than alternative technologies. Some countries will argue, however that even if a kilowatt-hour of electricity from the breeder is more costly, the promise of reduced dependence on fuel suppliers justifies the extra cost.

In order to understand the cost issue it is important to look at the elements that make up the cost of nuclear-produced electric power. The cost of the uranium in light-water reactors today is only about 10 percent of the bus bar (at the plant) cost of a kilowatt-hour of nuclear-produced electricity; 80 percent of the cost is capital, including interest on capital during construction. This means that every 1 percent increase in capital costs adds approximately the same amount to the cost of a kilowatt-hour of nuclear-produced electricity as an 8 percent increase in uranium cost. This ratio is important for the economics of the breeder, because its capital cost is expected to be significantly higher than that of light-water reactors. What the actual capital cost of breeders would turn out to be is highly uncertain. However, a recent Bechtel estimate of the cost of the French Superphénix design (made on the assumption that it is built in an unidentified country other than France or the United States) arrived at an additional capital increment of 35 percent. This increment yields a break-even uranium price of around $190 per pound in 1978 dollars.[12] Other cost estimates suggest that the capital cost of the breeder will be 25 to 75 percent greater than that of light-water reactors. Even at the low end of the range, the break-even U_3O_8 would be around $150 per pound.[13]

These and similar trade-off calculations that are often made usually assume that the breeder would not incur other costs higher than those of the light-water reactor. This is a doubtful assumption. For instance, in the breeder, the burn-up of fuel would be higher; this means a much higher load of fission products, much greater concentration of plutonium, and consequently, in all likelihood, an increase in reprocessing costs per kilogram of fuel by comparison with current estimates, which in turn are very much larger than those assumed earlier. Furthermore, fuel rods that contain a higher proportion of plutonium (as is optional for a breeder) will have higher fabrication costs than those that do not.

A line of argument supporting the proposition that the breeder might become economically competitive (neglecting its proliferation-related costs) early in the twenty-first century asserts the following: U.S. and world energy demand will continue to grow, although at a reduced rate from that of the several decades before 1973. World recoverable oil and gas resources are likely to be substantially depleted by the year 2000. Although there are large coal resources in the world, environmental constraints may seriously restrict the extent to which the use of coal can be increased. There is no assurance that any major new energy source will be competitive and be introduced on a large scale by, say, the year 2025. Estimates (including those cited earlier) that there is plenty of low-cost uranium may be wrong; besides, there is the question of security of supply (discussed below). The most confidently available "backstop" technology, then, is the plutonium breeder, with its fabled capacity to extract fifty times as much energy from a pound of uranium as the light-water reactor can.

There are quite a few assumptions in this line of reasoning, each of which is questionable. For instance, consider the long-term prospects of energy demand. An extrapolation of the U.S. post-World War II energy growth rate through 1973, which was around 4 percent annually, would yield an energy demand in the year 2000 of about 210 quads (10^{15} BTU). Typical projections today, however, yield energy-demand estimates for that year of about half as much. To be sure, there are good reasons to expect electricity demand to grow more rapidly than the demand for other types of energy, because the anticipated depletion of oil and gas supplies will increase their prices more rapidly than that of electricity. But there are several troublesome aspects to many of these projections. One is that they are for the most part obscure on the effect of increases in energy prices on incentives for making energy-saving innovations, a phenomenon that could have a powerful effect over the course of three or four decades.[14] Second, many recent projections have assumed a basic growth rate for the United States and the world economy that does not take adequate account of demographic changes and the clear decline in expected per captia economic growth rates—at least in the developed world. To be sure, much can change in capital formation and in technological innovation—but not in the size of the work force—over the next forty years, but on present evidence, a modest energy growth demand—around 2.5 percent or less—seems most likely for the world; for the United States, an energy growth rate lower than this is likely.[15]

For U.S. electricity, these factors suggest a 3 to 4 percent annual increase, roughly doubling by the year 2000. Continued growth of electricity demand at this rate—i.e., with a doubling time of twenty-four years—would, of course, eventually put a large strain on coal and uranium resources. If environmental constraints are put on the growth of coal use, nuclear electric power would grow more rapidly, as it is scheduled to do through the 1980s. But only if (1) the uranium supply is much less than estimated by the Department of Energy, and (2) constraints on coal use and other assumptions force rapid depletion of uranium would the price of U_3O_8 perhaps exceed, early in the twenty-first century, the threshold level at which the breeder becomes cost-competitive. In anticipation of this prospect, utilities might introduce some breeders earlier.

It is important to note that economic signals would tell us which path we were on long before large-scale commitment to breeders was needed. We need not decide *now* what technologies to deploy in the twenty-first century. Moreover, it has been too seldom noticed how little difference the introduction of the plutonium breeder makes to the consumption of uranium for many years. The rate of breeder introduction might be constrained by the perceived "downside" risk of loss from premature introduction of a new technology. It might also be constrained by the available stockpile of plutonium. Its subsequent growth rate could be limited by the breeding rate of plutonium in the first generation of breeders. These possible limits on the breeder-introduction rate suggest that other fuels (including uranium) would continue to be in demand.

This analysis suggests that, from the perspective of energy economics, the breeder should be viewed in the same way that other new energy technologies, with different associated uncertainties, are viewed—fusion, solar, oil shale, enhanced oil recovery, coal gasification and liquefaction, improved thermal reactors, and the like. Contrary to the view held by some, there is no need now for commitment to the breeder; there is ample time to choose among the candidates for the twenty-first century.

Notes

1. The prospect that the cost of reprocessing in light-water reactors was likely to be uneconomic, and that at best reprocessing could produce only a very small saving in electricity cost, was first seriously raised by Albert Wohlstetter et al. in "Moving Toward Life in a Nuclear Armed Crowd?" *Pan Heuristics*, April 1976. This conclusion was also reached in *Nuclear Power: Issues and Choices* (New York: The Ford Foundation and MITRE Corporation, 1977), and later in the report to the American Physical Society of its task force on nuclear fuel goals and waste management, *Review of Modern Physics*, vol. 50, no. 1, Part II (January 1978).

2. In Germany and Japan, reprocessing must now meet legal requirements for waste disposal. The main safety barrier for the long-term storage of waste is geologic isolation, however, and this is true whether it is the spent fuel rods or the wastes left after reprocessing that are to be stored. Recently the refusal of the government of Lower Saxony to approve the Gorleben reprocessing plant has indefinitely deferred reprocessing plans in Germany.

3. *Energy Daily*, July 6, 1977. There is a considerable spread of estimates of reserves. An American Academy of Sciences panel, using very narrow criteria, has estimated resources of 1.8 million tons, while an advisory group to the Nuclear Regulatory Commission has estimated 5 million tons.

The Department of Energy "forward cost" category excludes certain important economic cost categories, including return on investment; $50 per pound "forward cost" may correspond to about $85 per pound long-run marginal cost.

4. *Nuclear Power: Issues and Choices*, (New York: The Ford Foundation and MITRE Corporation, 1977). Also, DeVerle P. Harris, "Informational and Conceptual Issues of Uranium Resources and Potential Supply," Workshop on Energy Information, Stanford University, December 1977.

5. Vince Taylor, "The Myth of Uranium Security," *Pan Heuristics*, April 25, 1977.

6. Letter from Lee V. Gossik, Executive Director for Operations, Nuclear Regulatory Commission, to Congressman James G. Martin (undated). The date of the estimate is June 6, 1977.

7. Draft Report of the Task Force for Review of Nuclear Waste Management, Department of Energy, February 1978.

8. The projected uranium consumption during the lifetime of the reactors installed through the year 2000 would be around 2.3 million tons of U_3O_8, with no burn-up improvement. With probable improvements, this total might be around 1.8 million tons.

9. "Nuclear Fuel Cycle Requirements," OECD, February 1978, Paris.

10. DeVerle P. Harris, "World Uranium Resources and Potential Supply," paper prepared for the NASAP/INFCE Summer Study at Aspen, Colorado, August 1978. Using several estimation methods, all highly speculative, the author, who is Director of Mineral Economics in the Department of Mining and Geological Engineering at the University of Arizona, estimates that the amount of world uranium resources available at under $50 per pound of U_3O_8 is greater than 13 million tons.

11. Ibid. On this estimate, which assumes a 30 percent reduction in uranium consumption per kilowatt-hour of nuclear electricity consumed after the year 2000, total uranium required through the year 2025 would be around 12 million tons. This would fuel the then existing reactors through their remaining lifetimes.

12. These estimates assume a light-water reactor capital cost of $950/KW$_e$ in 1978 dollars, a capital charge rate of 12 percent, and consumption of 133 tons of U3O8 annually.

13. For a careful analysis of breeder economics consistent with this estimate, see Brian Chow, "Economic Comparison of Breeders and Light Water Reactors," Pan Heuristics, prepared for the Arms Control and Disarmament Agency, July 23, 1979.

14. "U.S. Energy Demand: Some Low Energy Futures," *Science*, 200, no. 4338 (April 14, 1978) pp. 142-152.

15. William W. Hogan, "Energy Demand Forecasts: Comparisons and Sensitivities," Energy Modeling Forum, Stanford University, August 1978 (processed).

13
Measures to Enhance
Security of Supply

The prospect that uranium and enrichment services will be available in abundance and are more likely than not to be relatively cheap for a considerable period of time should be of some comfort to those nations that do not have indigenous sources of uranium or enrichment technology, but it may not meet their concerns about the political distribution of these resources. The 1973 oil crisis made many governments keenly aware of their vulnerability to cutoffs of energy supplies. Although the economic argument for the use of recycled plutonium as fuel is increasingly perceived to be weak, the argument based on security of supply continues to have powerful political appeal.

One worry expressed is that the number of major sources of uranium today is small, and the number of suppliers of enrichment services is even smaller. By the mid-1980s, the United States will still have about two-thirds of the non-Communist world's enrichment capacity. The U.S. action (taken in 1974) of ceasing to accept new contracts for enrichment services is often cited as evidence of the vulnerability of many countries to this critical resource. So also, more recently, is the U.S. Nuclear Nonproliferation Act of 1978. As characterized by more than a few observers from abroad, it is a unilateral act by the United States to change the rules under which other nations may obtain U.S. nuclear fuel services and technology. Canada has also adopted a tighter policy on nuclear exports and is restricting uranium exports in order to assure adequate supplies for domestic use. It appears that Australia will become a significant exporter of uranium, but internally its export policy is controversial and that policy's future is not entirely predictable. South African supplies might be disrupted by internal unrest. To be sure, further exploration is likely to result in many more producer nations, but to the importers the market looks highly concentrated and the important producers appear unreliable. These concerns enhance the attraction of recycling in light-water reactors, introduction of the breeder, and acquisition of an isotope separation technology.

Just as the widely held beliefs about fuel-cycle economics or resource scarcity have been unwarranted, so too should arguments on fuel vulnerability be regarded skeptically. The point is often made by Europeans and Japanese that the United States, with access to large amounts of oil, gas, and uranium, can afford to forgo reprocessing and the breeder, but that others cannot. But in terms of the potential vulnerability of supply, there are several significant differences between oil and nuclear fuel. For example, because of the high cost of petroleum and petroleum storage, commercial oil inventories seldom cover more than several weeks of consumption. At considerable cost, the United States is building a strategic oil reserve of 1 billion barrels, an amount equivalent to around 120 days of total oil imports or double that number of days of imports from the unpredictable Middle East. Other Organization for Economic Cooperation and Development (OECD) countries have similar programs. In contrast, the cost of enriched nuclear fuel contributes much less to the overall cost of electricity, and nuclear fuel is much less costly to store. For instance, holding a five-year supply of nuclear fuel would add only about 10 percent to the cost of a kilowatt-hour of electricity (at a 10 percent average real cost of capital). Nuclear fuel, therefore, presents a very much less acute problem of supply vulnerability than oil. This fact seems to be recognized; for example, Euratom reported that its member countries had 5,600 tonnes (metric tons) of enriched fuel on hand as of January 1977, enough to meet their programmed needs for about five years on the average.[1]

Recycling in light-water reactors has also been argued for on the grounds of reduced dependence on imports for countries lacking indigenous supplies. It was shown earlier that the savings to the year 2000 would be modest—around 20 percent. This will not bring anything like nuclear fuel independence, still less independence in the total electricity sector, and even less in the total energy sector.[2] Nonetheless, a reduction in import dependence, other things being equal, would to some extent be useful to any resource-poor country. But other things are not equal; in particular, the risks from stimulating wider access to nuclear explosive materials are greater.

The focus of the energy-independence argument, however, is not on recycling in light-water reactors but on the plutonium breeder. For example, it is said that deferral of the use of plutonium is easy for the United States, with its large reserves of energy from conventional sources. A European commentator has asserted that "breeders are the only technology now available that provide practically unlimited energy once oil is depleted."[3] The suggestion that breeders are "now available" is misleading. In a sense, they have been available for over a quarter-century; the *first* nuclear electric power was produced in a breeder reactor, the EBR-I, in 1951; but, that was not *economic* electric power, nor is breeder-produced electricity competitive today. Out of the six principal breeder research and development programs in the world might come electricity at a competitive price; then again, maybe not.

Of course, a government might be willing to pay a premium for electricity in order to gain some security of supply (though if the premium were, say, 50 percent, the economic burden would be heavy indeed). What is not widely understood is that the breeder could do little for energy independence for a long time to come. In the first place, breeders are still in the research and development stage; they could not become commercially significant until after the year 2000. This is true not only of the U.S. breeder but of those of other nations. In the second place, the rate of breeder introduction abroad could be even slower than in the United States, because in most countries the stocks of plutonium could prove too small to permit a rapid expansion rate.[4] Finally, there are limits on the extent to which foreign utilities will put money at risk in a new technology. The history of the German nuclear energy program illustrates the limits of that central government's ability to make decisions affecting the utilities' choices.[5]

The net effect of these factors is to make the cumulative saving of uranium to the year 2025 rather modest (about 20-25 percent for an industrialized country such as West Germany). Even if the breeder proves to be economically competitive, this saving is less than might be realized over this same period from incremental improvements in the performance of light-water reactors. The impact on national *energy* independence would, of course, be much less. For Japan or for Germany, countries with substantial nuclear programs, the constraints on the rate of introduction of even a successful breeder development program would make it difficult for these countries to displace more than 10 percent of their energy consumption by the year 2025.[6]

In short, what the energy-independence argument for the breeder amounts to is a declaration that governments should commit themselves *now* to the wide circulation of nuclear explosive materials in order to achieve a reduction in primary resource use that would only begin to be significant more than forty years from now. The more reasonable course is not to stop all research and development on the breeder, but to do a comparable level of research and development on alternate nuclear and nonnuclear energy systems as well.

Suppose that the predictions of early depletion of oil and gas are correct, and that the use of nuclear power has been restricted. What then would be the economic consequences? The answer depends critically on the fact that the energy sector makes up a small part of the total economy — typically about 5 percent — and on the elasticity of substitution of labor and capital for energy within this economy. For plausible values of the elasticity of substitution, the economic cost is not high. For some typical values, a reduction in end-use consumption of energy of 30 percent would reduce the value of total output by around 1 to 3 percent.[7]

The focus on these analytic data is not intended to show that nuclear power is irrelevant to security of energy supply. Rather it is to show that the use of plutonium as a fuel not only is unlikely to produce much by way of energy independence for a long time to come, but also that if *security of access* to fuels in the face of external interruption of supplies is the goal, a large measure of such security can be obtained through other measures, more quickly and probably more cheaply.

For an international nuclear system to have the desirable properties sought, it is important that nations be assured of access to nuclear fuel at a fair price. In the absence of this security, the tendency to nuclear autarky is strong. But for most countries, nuclear autarky would take a very long time to achieve; to achieve it would leave them in a position of continued dependence on imports of fossil fuels for many years, and even then autarky would be costly, perhaps unattainable. Worse, it would create a more dangerous world. As observed above, however, security of supply in the face of most types of interruptions could be met by a policy of stockpiling low enriched fuel. A five-year supply could be kept at relatively low cost.

For the midterm, say from five to fifteen years into the future, the willingness of governments without indigenous resources to depend on the market is an empirical matter. Arguably the best assurance of supply is to have a competitive market with many sellers. Many countries are diversifying their purchases of uranium and of enrichment services (in the latter case making purchases from the Soviet Union and the French-organized consortium for uranium enrichment [Eurodif] as well as from the United States.) The certain expansion of the number of uranium producers will help to allay fears of insecurity of supply. And exploration for uranium in some geologically promising countries that do not have large proven reserves might be encouraged. In its way, the market is doing this, but results would be more rapid if a well-designed program of exploration were mounted.

A much more dangerous prospect is the spread of isotope separation technology. Moreover, several nations are planning to build enrichment plants. The hazards of this spread strengthen the case for building institutions to increase confidence in the availability of nuclear fuel without the necessity for the widespread installation of separation plants that can be converted to making weapons-grade materials.

One suggestion is the creation of "internationally controlled stockpiles of low enriched uranium . . . available for release under carefully defined conditions to countries in compliance with their nonproliferation undertakings."[8] In October 1977, President Carter announced U.S. willingness to study the creation of such a stockpile. Although in many ways not analogous, a "bank" for uranium would have one main similarity with a bank for money: it would employ the principle of fractional reserves. Instead of holding its own fuel stocks, each country could draw on a common reserve when supplies were needed.

The political acceptability of a bank would depend crucially on the terms under which "withdrawals" could be made. Its rules of operation, including the distribution of voting rights for determining conformance with these rules, would be a matter of great importance. To be acceptable to the major nuclear fuel importers, a system of weighted voting, akin to that of the International Monetary Fund, would probably be needed. The weighting would presumably have to favor these major industrial countries. The less developed countries would not welcome such weighted voting, but given their smaller participation, they would have little alternative. The International Fuel Bank (see p. 145) would not necessarily have to keep much fuel in its possession so long as it had adequate drawing rights from the countries that have fuel.

Other schemes have been proposed: the Acheson-Lilienthal report proposed a single international enterprise that would own and operate enrichment services and store spent fuel.[9] The more comprehensive and ambitious of such schemes are unlikely to win international acceptance — the world is not going to create an institution with a monopoly over so important a resource. The idea was rejected in 1946, and it would be rejected today. Other schemes include institutions to "stabilize" uranium or enrichment prices and are also of dubious worth. They could prove even more destabilizing to these markets than the actions of governments have been so far.

Notes

1. H. W. Schleicher and B. W. Sharpe, "The Euratom Safeguard System as a Regional Control System," paper delivered to the International Conference on Nuclear Power and Its Fuel Cycle, (Salzburg, Austria, May 1977).

2. Some countries will *increase* overall dependency by adopting nuclear power, because they must depend for many years on outside suppliers of spare parts and maintenance services. Iran, which has fossil fuels in abundance, is a case in point.

3. Karl Kaiser, "The Great Nuclear Debate," *Foreign Policy*, no. 30 (Spring 1978).

4. The use of enriched uranium could speed the start-up process, but

at additional cost. During this period, dependence on outside suppliers of enrichment services would continue.

5. Otto Keck, "Fast Breeder Reactor Development in West Germany: An Analysis of Government Policy," doctoral diss., (University of Sussex, June 1977).

6. A representative estimate assumes 60 GW_e nuclear capacity in the year 2000. The first breeder is assumed to be on-line in the year 2000. The early rate of introduction is constrained by the more stringent of two factors: the willingness of utilities to invest in a new and possibly risky technology, and the availability of plutonium as fuel. The latter is determined by the amount of plutonium produced in light-water reactors, by reprocessing capacity, and by the doubling rate of plutonium production. The other breeder characteristics assumed are initial fuel inventory of five tons fissile plutonium, a 0.65 capacity factor, and an annual breeding gain of 4 percent.

7. Based on unpublished calculations by Vince Taylor. See also Alan Manne and William Hogan, "Energy-Economy Interactions: The Fable of the Elephant and the Rabbit," in C. J. Hitch, ed., *Modeling Energy-Economy Interaction: Five Approaches* (1977), available from Resources for the Future, 1755 Massachusetts Avenue, N.W., Washington D.C. 20036.

8. Joseph S. Nye, "Nonproliferation: A Long-Term Strategy," *Foreign Affairs*, 56, no. 3 (April 1978), p. 615.

9. An analysis of several alternative systems is provided in Henry D. Jacoby and Thomas L. Neff, coprinicipal investigators, "Determinants of Nuclear Fuel Assurance and Strategies for Assured Supply of Low Enriched Uranium Fuel," Working Paper #1, MIT Energy Laboratory and The Center for International Studies, December 22, 1977, draft. For a far-reaching scheme, a modern version of the Acheson-Lilienthal proposal, see the Stanford Law School International Fuel Cycle Working Group paper, "Evaluation of a Proposal for an International Nuclear Fuel Authority," (Stanford Institute of Energy Studies, December 1978).

14
The Importance of Dealing
with the "Back End"

For many utilities and governments, much of the interest in the reprocessing of spent fuel is related to the need to dispose of accumulating spent fuel. Environmentalists opposing nuclear energy in a number of countries assert that, until long-term disposal arrangements are made for spent fuel, no more nuclear plants should be built; they charge, moreover, that the safety of long-term disposal has not yet been adequately demonstrated. In fact, long-term disposal arrangements have not been satisfactorily settled upon and nuclear fuel is accumulating in storage pools, located for the most part at reactor sites. The accumulation itself gives environmentalist opponents another point of leverage in blocking further construction.

The position adopted years ago by most of the world's nuclear industry was that the solution would be found in the recycling of the plutonium and uranium in the spent fuel, followed by incorporating the waste fission products in some suitable refractory form, probably a glass, and disposing of it in deep isolated storage. A number of questions have been raised about this strategy, however. For example, although reprocessing removes most of the long-lived radioactive plutonium, it substitutes shorter-lived elements (e.g., americium-243 and curium-244). The problem of isolating these elements from the environment is about the same for about the first 500-1,000 years; thereafter, it is somewhat reduced. Moreover, additional wastes that require isolation from the environment are generated in the recycling process, and wastes from the plutonium fuel of a recycle system have a higher heat output than wastes from uranium fuel in a once-through system.

Reprocessing would probably leave the waste problem no more manageable than it is with unreprocessed fuel, which could be dealt with simply by storing the rods in canisters—perhaps in retrievable form for the first several decades. This idea is not novel; the Canadians have been planning on storing fuel in this way for at least several decades before either reprocessing it or undertaking permanent dispositon. In the view of the Task Force for Review of Nuclear Waste Management in the Department of Energy, "No compelling argument could be found that chemical reprocessing of comercial spent fuel is required for safety in waste management."[1]

There is a "safety" problem, however, in simply leaving spent fuel stored indefinitely in many countries around the world. There could be circumstances of crisis in which the extraction of plutonium from the spent fuel would be undertaken. Removal of spent fuel would be a safeguard against this possibility.

The Carter administration recognized this principle in announcing in October 1977 that the United States is prepared to accept a limited amount of foreign spent fuel, when to do so would contribute to meeting nonproliferation goals. Return of spent fuel is not a novel concept; the Soviet Union in fact mandates the return of spent fuel from Eastern Europe. Although the United States would be doing something quite useful in accepting "a limited amount of spent fuel," what is needed is the creation of an international system for the management of spent fuel. President Carter's announcement is a step in the creation of such a system; a similar step by another country, say Canada, either parallel with the United States or, better, through joint action of the two governments, would help things along. International cooperation would also mitigate the objections to the acceptance of foreign spent fuel that are likely to be raised. Although the draft waste-management report released by the Department of Energy finds that "a majority of independent technical experts have concluded that high-level waste can be safely disposed in geological media," it states that some technical issues still need to be resolved and also points out that a National Waste Repository for permanent disposal may not be operational by 1985.[2] Although many environmentalists endorse the principle of the return of spent fuel to the United States on nonproliferation grounds, there will be opposition on the grounds that the long-term storage issue has not been fully resolved. There is a balancing of risks here; on balance it appears that *not* moving internationally on the spent fuel issue is more dangerous than moving.

Because the cost of extracting uranium and plutonium from spent fuel is likely to be as much as or more than the value of the recovered fuel, the spent fuel would have little or no present market value.[3] The current U.S. spent-fuel policy provides for a one-time fee charged at the time of delivery to cover the full cost of interim storage and subsequent permanent disposal. No credit is included for either the plutonium or uranium in the fuel. If at some point in the future, however, the United States should decide that commercial reprocessing can be done without serious proliferation risk, then the spent fuel could be returned for appropriate refund or other compensation.

Although for some countries, for example Japan, the accumulation of this fuel is an embarrassment, for others it could be an opportunity to profit by offering storage sites. Governments with spent fuel they want to be rid of should be able to contract with those who are willing to accept it (and who also meet a test of political stability) for a fee, with the transaction handled either bilaterally or through an international agency. In short, it is time to begin construction of one or more international organizations for the management of spent fuel.

Notes

1. Draft Report of Task Force for Review of Nuclear Waste Management, U.S. Department of Energy (February 1978), p. 7.
2. Ibid, pp. 2, 3.
3. If there were a futures market for plutonium, spent fuel might have a nonzero value, despite the reprocessing-cost barrier, on the expectation of a future price rise in uranium. Given the political risks involved, it would be a daring speculator willing to bet much on a long position in spent fuel.

15
Alternative Paths Examined

The most substantial of all bars to the acquisition of nuclear explosives is a sense of adequate security. Some countries are fortunate enough to possess it in large measure through an accident of geography or the lack of regional adversaries. For others, security lies in alliance ties, sometimes backed up by the presence of allied forces or even their nuclear weapons.

Some countries face only nonweapons states as their immediate rivals or adversaries. Where an adversary is powerful and threatening, the transfer of nonnuclear arms may help nonproliferation goals, particularly where the alternative is that the vulnerable party might develop nuclear arms. Governments in this position may move to acquire nuclear weapons or, perhaps implicitly, threaten to get them if they are not provided with adequate nonnuclear arms. Such bargaining threats should not, of course, be taken at face value but should be examined on their merits. In this light, collective security systems and arms transfers have merits that it has not been fashionable to recognize in the several years.

Some states, such as Taiwan and Pakistan, have adversaries that possess nuclear explosives as well. For protection against nuclear threats, a nonweapon state needs a security tie with a nuclear power. Nuclear guarantees, especially by the great powers, are of central importance for the security and stability of Europe and other regions as well as Japan. But it is evident that the capacity of a great power to deliver on its nuclear guarantee to an ally—for instance ours to Western Europe in the face of an overwhelming nonnuclear Soviet attack—depends on the nonimplementation of Article VI of the NPT, which calls for total nuclear disarmament by the nuclear powers. That such disarmament would remove incentives for nuclear armament everywhere is a position held both by those of utopian disposition and by those who want a reason for *not* forgoing nuclear explosives themselves. In fact, the probability of total nuclear disarmament in the world is virtually nonexistent, given the rivalries that exist for instance between the United States and the Soviet Union, China and the Soviet Union, or even India and China. It can hardly be seriously argued that nuclear disarmament by the United States or the Soviet Union, would make, say, the Germans, the Pakistanis, the Israelis, the South Koreans, or the Taiwanese feel more comfortable about their security. For some, the opposite would be true. Note the concern that Europeans have expressed that the U.S.-USSR strategic arms limitation agreements may erode the efficacy of U.S. nuclear guarantees to Europe; this attitude illuminates the destabilizing potential of such agreements. Alliance ties and nuclear guarantees provide important incentives for nonnuclear states to stay that way.

Sometimes, however, alliance support may be politically impossible. A case in point is South Africa, a country that is isolated internationally and rapidly acquiring nuclear capacities that could at any time be allocated to the development of explosives.

The Need for Clarity on Safeguards

The point has been made that governments can come very close to having bombs without violating safeguards. A clearer recognition of this fact underlay the recent changes in the U.S. position on nuclear nonproliferation policy. In one view, international safeguards are a mechanism of little effectiveness, a mechanism that has the side effect of legitimizing the transfer of dangerous technologies and materials. Under the present IAEA system, there are reasons for concern about the system's capacity to safeguard reactors reliably. On balance, however, the international safeguards system does have positive value.

For one thing, the system's functions of inspection and of material accountability monitoring are potentially useful technically. Constraints on the inspection budget, which have affected both the system's *modus operandi* and the degree of intrusiveness the inspection methods have so far permitted, have limited the effectiveness of this system, but a foundation exists on which to build. The system also provides a mechanism through which countries that are not violating international agreements can demonstrate that they are operating within the agreement.

Not everything is equally "safeguardable," however, in the sense that even perfect safeguards would not guarantee the "safety" of some activities. The operative concept here is that of critical time. Where the critical time from a civilian status to a military one is long, then the utility of safeguards can be high; where the critical time is short, the safeguards remain useful, but the situation is dangerous at best.

Light-water reactors operated on a once-through mode lend themselves to a reasonably effective inspection system. Fresh fuel is not an explosive material; refueling is a major operation and is done infrequently. Spent fuel, however, requires continuous monitoring (a practice not now followed by the IAEA but technically feasible) in order to assure that some fuel rods have not been removed for reprocessing. Heavy-water reactors present more of a problem. Their on-line refueling system means that to achieve high confidence in a safeguard-system continuous monitoring of both reactor operations and spent fuel is required.

Prospective safeguard systems for isotope separation plants should satisfy two objectives: one is assurance that the plant is producing only low enriched uranium; the other is timely detection of possible changes to the production of highly enriched material. The first requirement can scarcely be met if inspectors must stay outside of the plant fence, but it is not yet clear that concerns about industrial secrecy (or national security) will allow "inside the fence" monitoring. There should be some way of reconciling these two objectives. The requirement of timely detection varies strongly with technology. For diffusion plants of the type the United States has operated since World War II, the time required to switch from low enriched to high enriched material is measured in months; for centrifuges, the time is much shorter, on the order of weeks.

The French have claimed that, using their chemical isotope separation technology, the time required to produce highly enriched material is very long. Technical information for verifying this claim, however, has evidently not yet been made available to other governments. The upshot is that the "safeguardability" of isotope separation plants depends strongly on the technology used.

On the other hand, reprocessing plants present an essentially intractable safeguard problem, because a principal product is plutonium. Even if the plutonium product is blended with uranium in the plant, it can later be separated chemically with relative ease. Therefore, the assertion that reprocessing plants cannot be safeguarded is only a slight oversimplification. Strictly speaking, the assertion is oversimplified because there is some difference between the production of plutonium and the production of unirradiated MOX from which plutonium can readily be extracted.

In sum, even for those activities for which safeguards can make a significant difference, e.g., monitoring spent fuel storage, there is a need to expand and improve the existing system. But the limits to safeguards for those activities for which the critical time is short also need to be recognized.

The Tension Between Universality and Discrimination

Universal principles have the great merit of generating wise legitimacy. Prohibitions against commercial use of plutonium or highly enriched uranium anywhere, against international transfers of reprocessing technology, and against all "peaceful" nuclear explosions are examples of proposed universal rules in the nuclear sector.

The problem with universal rules is that they conform poorly to a diverse reality. This diversity is explicitly recognized in the NPT, which incorporates the distinction between weapons and nonweapons states. When the NPT was being negotiated, many nonweapons governments expressed concern that this distinction would lead to their being commercially disadvantaged, and some expressed resentment at the implied status distinction. This response led to Article IV, the effect of which is partly to eliminate the distinction that was the basis for having the NPT in the first place.

Reality in the world today includes large industrial powers some of which have nuclear weapons and some of which, such as Germany and Japan, do not; rapidly developing countries with aspirations for wealth and power in the world, such as Brazil and Iran; smaller rapidly developing countries such as South Korea and Taiwan; and many small and poor countries with less promising prospects for growth. The prospects for economic use of nuclear energy differ widely; so does political stability. Moreover, some countries have embarked on programs to reprocess spent fuel and to develop breeder reactors while others have not. This fact, together with a desire by the United States not to disrupt relations with important allies, has led to U.S. approval of some existing projects, e.g. the operation of the Japanese reprocessing plant at Tokai Mura using spent fuel of U.S. origins. There clearly is a problem in drawing lines. For example, the Nuclear Nonproliferation Act of 1978 makes a distinction between criteria for approval of transfers of fuel of U.S. origin applicable to facilities in operation and distinguishes between arrangements made before and after March 10, 1978; the latter must meet more stringent standards. The cases that have arisen suggest that it will not be easy to hold this line.[1]

How can the reality of large differences among states be reconciled with the important principle of nondiscrimination? Global undertakings pose this tension in the most acute form. To the extent that actions can be made bilateral or treated on a regional basis — as in the Treaty for the Prohibition of Nuclear Weapons in Latin America — implementation may be easier. But there should be no illusions that this treaty is without defect. Not only has it not been ratified by two of the most important Latin American powers, Argentina and Brazil, but its Article 18 permits "explosions of nuclear devices for peaceful purposes" by any of the contracting parties. In this regard it is less restrictive than the NPT. On the other hand, consider the inherent obstacles to agreements that build on the basic distinction incorporated in the NPT, that between weapons and nonweapons states. That distinction suggests that activities closely related to the production of nuclear weapons, e.g., work on the plutonium breeder, the operation of centrifuge enrichment plants, and the operation of large research reactors, be limited to weapons states, on the grounds that these countries have nuclear explosives anyway. But such restrictions would be strongly resisted by at least those major industrial powers that have become major nuclear technology centers, including

West Germany and Japan. If it turns out not to be feasible to limit ready access to nuclear explosive materials to weapons states, the distinction between weapons states and nonweapons states will be sharply eroded. The consequences would be uncertain but quite possibly disastrous.

The problem in drawing lines that will win substantial international agreement and at the same time be stable is reflected in proposals that would confine dangerous activities to weapons states plus the major nuclear technology centers, say, Germany, Japan, and Canada. What about the other members of Euratom, or countries such as Sweden and Switzerland? And for that matter, aspirations, if not present competency, are sure to cause Brazil, among others, to want to be inside rather than outside of this club. Shortsightedness on this point is likely to prove costly.

The problem as posed is certainly difficult, perhaps impossible, to solve. But in addressing it we should be mindful of the fact that much that is said to be inevitable in the world—including in its nuclear sector—may not come to pass. Thus earlier predictions that nuclear energy would be virtually costless, that many nations would have nuclear weapons by 1970, or that commercial breeder reactors would be operating today, have proved false. This may also be the fate of contemporary assertions that current breeder developments will inevitably be carried forward, or that isotope separation plants and reprocessing plants will certainly become widely distributed. After all, the last several years have seen a major change in U.S. nuclear policy, a reversal of position by France and by West Germany on the export of reprocessing plants, and great slippage in projections of installed nuclear capacity by the years 1985 and 2000.

This record of change bears crucially on the prospect for evolving a set of rules for the use of nuclear energy that will avert the worst dangers and be nonetheless reasonably stable. Some of the most vexing problems may ease.

Four Future Paths for the World

Consider four possible paths that the world might follow in the next several decades.

Path 1: Strengthening the Distinction Between Weapons States and Nonweapons States

If this path is followed, the NPT would in effect have to be reinterpreted as meaning that certain technologies and materials would not be situated in nonweapon states, in conformance with the first principle for a safer international system (as previously described). Under this regime, full-scope safeguards would be adopted; institutions would be created to help assure the supply of nuclear fuel to countries that adhere to their nonproliferation undertakings; and help in the management of spent fuel would be provided as well.[2]

Following this path does not imply that, for example, all governments would soon — say, at the end of the International Fuel Cycle Evaluation — agree to such a change in the rules; this is very unlikely to happen. Nor does it imply that the Japanese will stop reprocessing at Tokai Mura or the Germans at Wak, or that national breeder programs in either place (or those in Britain, France, the United States, or the Soviet Union) will be cancelled. It does imply both a lessening of interest over time in the use of plutonium fuel, on economic grounds, and a heightened recognition of the dangers of plutonium and of the spread of isotope separation technology.

Nor does following this path imply total conformity by all governments. Some would probably choose to ignore such distinctions and seek to adopt technologies that would enable them to move quickly to acquire weapons, and some other nations might even skip the formalities and simply acquire the weapons. They might do so if other nations were unwilling or unable to provide them with enough security or to exert sufficient economic, political, or military influence to prevent them from going ahead. The assumption here, however, is that a general international consensus emerges on the utility of making operational distinctions between weapons and nonweapons states.

Path 2: Establishing and Building on the Distinction Between Industrialized and Nonindustrialized States

This distinction has the great virtue of accommodating a

number of important realities: that Japan and Germany have breeder programs and reprocessing technology; that Japan, with U.S. concurrence, is having some spent fuel reprocessed in France and Britain; that countries such as Sweden and Switzerland are also having fuel reprocessed; and that plutonium recycling and the breeder are less suited to the economies of the less developed countries than to those of the industrialized countries. The wide adoption of full-scope safeguards and the development of institutions for assuring fuel supply and helping with spent-fuel management, as under Path 1, would also have to be adopted under this path. This distinction is also consistent with that of the Suppliers' Group, which developed a common position on nuclear exports. It would draw a line between the countries of the North and those of the South, i.e., between the industrializing countries and "the others," the latter presumably including South Korea, Taiwan, Pakistan, the Philippines, and Argentina, but not Brazil, which is to receive the full fuel cycle from Germany. Among others, Argentina will not accept being on the "wrong" side of the line. It is certain that the Argentinians have their own thoughts about being denied the nuclear technologies being transferred to Brazil. In short, there is no clear place to draw the line between the industrialized (or "stable") states and the nonindustrialized (or "unstable") states. All of the less developed countries seek to leave that condition and many are succeeding. Hardly any government, no matter how shaky, can accept being labeled as "unstable." Nor can other nations easily afford to do the labeling.

Path 3: Muddling Along

Muddling is often the solution to seemingly intractable situations, and more than one kind of muddling can occur. One version might look like a *de facto* version of Path 2 without much visibility being accorded the distinction between stable versus unstable states. It would include acceptance on the part of the industrialized countries of limits on transfers of isotope separation reprocessing and breeder technology to the less industrialized countries, but it would be less restrictive in such transfers among these countries. Diplomatic and economic pressure would be put on countries outside of the "club" to forgo building facilities of these types. Full-scope safeguards would be adopted generally.

If, however, a version of muddling develops that finds Britain and France accepting spent fuel from all interested countries and then returning the plutonium, the barriers to weapons will effectively have been sharply reduced. Such a lack of cohesion among the suppliers could reinforce those outside of the "club" in the view that they should create their own indigenous capabilities, despite pressures not to do so. If such trade in dangerous technologies is permitted among the Euratom countries, Japan, and a few selected "others," while being more or less informally denied to everyone else (as in the agreement in the nuclear supplier club), erosion is certain to occur.

Path 4: Abandoning the Nonproliferation Regime

If the world lands on this path, it is most likely to be as a consequence of "muddling through." International diplomacy is probably capable of preventing a spectacular blowup of the present system, in which, for example, nations withdraw from the NPT in the 1980s and several undertake visible weapons programs. But perhaps a spectacular collapse would be less costly to the world than the gradual emergence of a highly dangerous situation obscured by ritualized inspections and governmental assurances that really all is well.

Notes

1. Joseph S. Nye Jr., Statement before the Subcommittee on International Economic Policy and Trade of the House Committee on International Relations, October 3, 1978. Published in Department of State Bulletin, vol. 79, no. 2022, January 1979.

2. For a discussion of the norms of a nonproliferation regime, see the remarks by Joseph S. Nye, Deputy to the Under Secretary of State, to the Uranium Institute, London, July 12, 1978.

16
Creating and Strengthening Institutions

Much of the discussion so far has dealt with the need for strengthening existing international institutions and the need for building certain new ones. We should harbor no illusions about how effective improved institutions can be if weapon-usable material is widely circulating in commerce throughout the world, but improved institutions might help to avert dire outcomes.

Institutional Initiatives

Several possibly useful initiatives might be taken.

Attending to fuel assurances

1. In order to increase confidence in supply security, and as an alternative to the much more dangerous national enrichment plants, the creation of enrichment consortia with plants located in politically stable states, operated under continuous safeguards, should be encouraged over the long term—that is, after the period of the enrichment "glut" that will exist through the 1980s. If their costs are competitive, or nearly so, enrichment plants designed to produce low enriched material should be encouraged: they can be safeguarded; and their lead time for conversion to the production of highly enriched uranium is substantial.

2. An International Fuel Bank might be created. One such bank might not be large enough to meet demands from large countries such as Japan or West Germany, but it could meet the needs of smaller ones.

3. Better information on the extent of world uranium resources

would be of great value. Promoting this public good suggests the usefulness of an international program to help acquire better information.

4. Fuel-cycle centers might be created in the weapons states (although certain activities might be located in nonweapons states, as discussed above). This is, in effect, the function performed today by countries that provide enrichment services. Other concepts for fuel-cycle centers have been proposed, including the use of the thorium-U-233 cycle in fuel-cycle centers, which would export denatured U-233 fuel to locations that employ only burner reactors and would, moreover, require the return of the plutonium-containing spent fuel.[1] Some object to the creation of such a two-part system on the grounds that it may seem inequitable to governments outside the energy centers. This suggests that financial inequities at least should be minimized by setting up arrangements for sharing the economic benefits — and costs — of such fuel-cycle centers.

Establishing International Arrangements to Manage Spent Fuel

Such international arrangements might be established through bilateral agreements for the return of spent fuel, regional agreements for the management of spent fuel and waste (e.g., within Euratom), or the assumption of the management function by either the IAEA or a new international institution invested specifically with this responsibility.

Stimulating International Cooperation in Certain Types of Nuclear Research

1. International cooperation on ways of making safer fuel cycles is under way through INFCE. INFCE should stimulate the additional research that will need to be continued well beyond its own lifetime.

2. By now it is evident that the wide distribution of research reactors, some of which produce large amounts of plutonium (as in the CIRUS reactor in India), and some of which use highly enriched uranium, should be stopped. Current efforts to substitute low enriched uranium are commendable but will not solve the problem altogether. Activities that cannot be made adequately safe, including the conduct of criticality experiments, should be concen-

trated in a small number of centers preferably located in weapons states (in accordance with Path 1) but at least should be limited to stable, industrial states such as West Germany or Japan (in accordance with Path 2).

Improving Means of Detecting and Interpreting Moves from a Legal State

1. Several IAEA functions need strengthening: the continuous monitoring of spent fuel needs to be instituted and continuous controls on enrichment plants need to be introduced to assure that only low enriched fuel is being produced. Enrichment-plant monitoring can hardly be managed effectively when all controls and inspectors must remain outside the plant fence, and no satisfactory system has yet been proposed. Some way of effectively monitoring a facility that maintains security on technical details (which is important for security or commerical reasons) must be developed.

2. National means of verification (or intelligence) need to be made as effective as possible. These means are much more likely to be successful in detecting and interpreting danger signals than is the IAEA system; furthermore, they are likely to be the basis on which key responses will be fashioned by governments. The IAEA system has the potential and complementary virtue of providing information that will be widely believed in the international arena.

Attending to the Health of Existing Security Ties

There can be little doubt that the erosion of collective security ties in the non-Communist world has increased incentives to acquire nuclear weapons. Preserving these ties, and reversing the erosion where possible, is important for many reasons, not least in order to help prevent the emergence of more weapons states.

Could Adoption of New Rules Make an Important Difference?

An assumption, often made explicit in the nuclear industry's opposition to changes in the international nuclear rules, is that any government can get explosives if it wants them — in short, that it is too late for technical restrictions to play a role other than in protecting against terrorists. The belief, held more often by technologists than by those who have greater familiarity with the working of politics, that governments will or will not go for the bomb in a clear and unambiguous way is not well supported by evidence. The evidence among the twenty-odd countries that by now could have had nuclear weapons (most of whom have, so far, elected to abstain) shows a much more complex pattern. It reveals a tendency toward incrementalism, toward creating options rather than toward working on consistent long-term aims.

This finding recognizes that there are several alternative paths to a bomb besides the use of plutonium from power reactors. In many countries, there would be high political costs in choosing a course identified as moving toward a bomb—especially if this move were in violation of agreements not to do so. In these countries, the government, or even the officials of a bureau, might take additional steps beyond those integral to civilian uses of nuclear energy to shorten the lead time to explosives, but the steps that would be taken would depend on the government's assessment of risks and benefits—including the consequences of violating the international rules to which the government has adhered. For example, if the agreed rules limited further international sale and stigmatized indigenuous development of large research reactors, then the building of a plutonium production reactor would be hard to conceal; it would risk unambiguous interpretation as a deliberate program of explosives production. This interrelationship sheds useful light on the assertion that, with extensive preparations prior to diversion, the chemical separation of plutonium from spent fuel would add little time or effort to the other steps needed to acquire explosives. A similar argument has been made with respect to enrichment technologies.

Among other things, this argument misses the point that these preparations may be sharply constrained by existing agreements and by a concern for maintaining secrecy. The problem faced by a country constrained in the ways described above, if it then decides to make bombs, is not simply one of risking IAEA detection of violations and subsequent sanctions by the suppliers of nuclear technology and fuel. For most governments contemplating moves toward the bomb, such sanctions will not be the chief deterrent; rather, these countries will be deterred by the potential responses of regional adversaries and the great powers to signals that they have undertaken a bomb program. Evidence might be available to others through intelligence channels that an internal decision had been taken to acquire nuclear explosive materials; signs of construction of a production reactor, enrichment facilities, or a reprocessing plant might be visible to the various national intelligence networks and might trigger unwanted responses. To be sure, some of these facilities could be small in size. Even so, against national intelligence systems—in contrast with IAEA inspection—they might be vulnerable to detection.

The length of the lead times involved, measured from the beginning of construction of such facilities, suggests the problem that governments contemplating such moves might face. It is important to recognize two points in this connnection. One is that the time, difficulty, and cost of making a bomb depend on where one starts. Objections that it would be uneconomic for governments to use material from research reactors to build bombs neglect what is relevant: the marginal cost of moving from a legal, possibly safeguarded state. The second point is that detection is a function of the elapsed time after leaving a legal state. The signals are likely to be deliberately suppressed. Therefore, estimates of critical time cannot be represented by a single number, but it is clear that the probability of being detected increases with time and with the extent of the departure from a legal status.

Examining the Cases

The importance of the legal starting point can be illustrated by considering several possibilities.[2]

Case 1. A nonweapons state has access to plutonium or highly enriched uranium in metallic form and has the facilities for shaping it for criticality experiments or for fabricating highly concentrated fissile fuel. In this case, if work on the nonnuclear components of a bomb has been completed, the critical time is nearly zero.

Case 2. Here, the starting point is the legitimate possession of plutonium and highly enriched uranium in nonmetallic forms such as plutonium nitrate or dioxide in, say, fuel assemblies or in spent fuel, or uranium alone in the form of highly enriched uranium hexaflouride. This case further assumes that reprocessing plants or enrichment plants of any type are legitimized — in effect, that state into which the evolution of the nuclear industry has been taking the world, the state that has been put in question. Under these conditions, the critical time to rework material to weapon-ready form is only days to weeks. Six months to a year are needed, however, for preparation of the rework facilities and nuclear components; if such facilities are themselves a violation, then critical time is several months to a year.

Case 3. Civilian status is limited to materials no nearer to use in explosives than mixed-oxide fuel (MOX) or low enriched uranium. These materials might be shipped from outside or produced in a sanctioned reprocessing plant designed for coprocessing. This status would ban isotope separation plants that can be converted quickly to producing highly enriched uranium from low enriched uranium, or reprocessing plants that can produce a separate plutonium stream. The critical time would be several months to a year for the construction of a spent-fuel reprocessing "laboratory" (plus the extra days or weeks needed to rework the material). The protection offered under this case, however, could be subverted by changing the coprocessing plant flows to provide a pure plutonium stream.

Case 4. Civilian status is defined as including light- and heavy-water reactors, gas reactors, or research reactors using slightly enriched or natural uranium fuel only once, with safeguarded spent-fuel storage. This is the benchmark case described earlier. The critical time would be roughly eighteen months — time enough for the construction of a facility to extract plutonium from hot spent fuel, followed by several weeks to a month to process material if experienced, expert personnel are available, or many months to a year if they are not.

Case 4a. In a variant of Case 4, civilian status might be limited to materials that are harder to handle than unirradiated MOX. In this case (as in the CIVEX proposal) only irradiated or "spiked" MOX would be permitted. The critical time is longer than in Case 3 (but the cost of handling nuclear fuel is increased). By comparison with the Case 4, the critical time is shorter, especially allowing for decay of radiation in fresh fuel stored before use.

Case 5. Civilian status as in Case 4, but the path to the military status chosen is the construction of large reactors to make plutonium, together with separation facilities. (Large plutonium-producing research reactors are assumed to be excluded in the civilian status.) The critical time here is upwards of five years.

Case 6. Civilian status as in Case 4, but the path to the military status chosen is the construction of an isotope separation plant to produce highly enriched uranium. The critical time is five years or more.

The conclusion to be drawn from these examples is that the variants for the benchmark case have critical times of over a year. (Even if the construction of a reprocessing plant were judged to have a high probability of going undetected, the critical time would be at least several weeks.) This is distinctly superior to the prospects for early detection with Cases 1, 2, and 3.

The benchmark case and its variants exclude the wide distribution of isotope separation facilities and large plutonium-producing reactors. Until recently, enrichment facilities were confined to the weapons states but they are now available on a small scale in the Netherlands, Japan, and South Africa, with Brazil scheduled to join the list. The URENCO consortium—Britain, West Germany, and the Netherlands—is a multinational arrangement stemming from the joint participation of several governments, one of which is a weapons state. Such multinational arrangements should generally be encouraged as an alternative to national plants. (Unhappily, the technology being used by the consortium is that of centrifuges, a technology that is especially troublesome from the standpoint of critical time.)

Removal of spent fuel to safeguarded storage sites is necessary in Cases 4 through 6.

Finally, the possibility that Case 4a, in which a radiation barrier is incorporated in fresh fuel, could approximate the benchmark case needs to be explored further. Given (1) the preferences of governments for having an adequate stockpile of fresh fuel on hand and (2) the decay of the radiation barrier, this does not seem likely.

No reactor technology that is significantly different from those now in use will be introduced on a sizable scale until the year 2000 at the earliest. Two additional cases, however, hold interest for the future.

Case 7. Use of uranium-233 denatured with uranium-238 or low enriched uranium (as in Case 4) outside of the internationally controlled energy centers. Enrichment technology permitting quick conversion to the production of highly enriched uranium and reprocessing plants would be similarly restricted outside of such centers. The critical time would probably be measured in many months, to construct a facility to extract the plutonium from hot spent fuel, or years, to build the isotope separation facilities needed to separate uranium-233 from uranium-238.

Case 8. Widespread distribution of fast breeder reactors, with the use of coprocessing and the international shipment of MOX. This case corresponds to Case 3 above (or Case 4a if only irradiated fuels are fabricated)—and it has a critical time of several months to a year.

Furthermore, in the future the spread of enrichment technologies could lead to a widespread reduction of critical times, apart from what happens with the commercial circulation of plutonium. Certainly, if wide distribution of plutonium becomes the norm, whether separated or in MOX, critical times are likely to be too short to provide much warning of moves to make explosives. Finally, schemes to extend uranium resources by adopting some variant of the thorium cycle (operated on a denatured cycle), or by using plutonium breeders with radioactive fresh fuel, may also offer extended critical times, but it is not yet clear how much additional time is involved or what the costs of such systems would be.

This evaluation illustrates the importance of making the legal starting point a circumstance requiring the use of configuration of institutions and technologies no less vulnerable to conversion to weapons production than the benchmark case, which presents the potential bomb builder with either an isotopic barrier or the necessity of dealing with intensely radioactive materials. With an agreed prohibition on isotope separation facilities, or at least on those with a short critical time, and with an agreed ban on reprocessing facilities, the starting point would be the construction of these facilities. The critical time would then be many months — although usable warning time to others might be a good deal less.

The issue is not whether agreements on fuel-cycle limitations would prevent an advanced industrial country at the level of a

Japan or a Germany from being able to acquire nuclear explosives. Clearly not; for these countries, the incentives dominate. The technical and military requirements that weapons programs would have to meet would be very demanding, however, even for such industrial giants as these. For many other nations, even with their less ambitious goals, developing usable explosives, delivery systems, command and control, and the like will not be easy.

The question remains, what is the value of possible gains in warning time? Clearly no simple answer can be given. History abounds with examples of warnings that were ignored, but it also records many examples where responses to early signals prompted effective action. Suffice it to say that signals giving months—or even days or weeks—of notice of moves toward making bombs will usually be worth a lot more than no warning at all.

A final question is the extent of reliance that should be placed on international institutions for the management of nuclear explosive materials. If the alternative is wide distribution of these materials under national control, then the political barriers represented by, say, joint ownership by several governments of plutonium or highly enriched uranium would be preferred by many people, even though these barriers might be substantial in some cases. But simply to attach the labels "international" or "multinational" to the conduct of such dangerous activities does not necessarily imply much of a political barrier. The words "control" or "ownership" can mean many different things, as can the word "safeguard." These words may mean little more than an acquiescence to national programs; they may even offer legitimation for them.

Notes

1. Harold A. Feiveson and Theodore B. Taylor, "Security Implications of Alternative Nuclear Futures," *Bulletin of the Atomic Scientists*, vol. 32 (December 1976).

2. These illustrative cases are taken from Albert Wohlstetter et al., *Swords from Plowshares* (Chicago: University of Chicago Press, 1979).

17
In Conclusion

The foregoing discussion suggests several reasons for the resistance to the U.S. initiatives: the nuclear industry has been deeply committed to recycling and the use of plutonium as fuel; the once-through fuel cycle is not seen as "credible" by many; the changes in U.S. enrichment policy have raised doubts about our reliability as a fuel supplier; and we have done little to help with the growing spent-fuel problem.[1] Moreover, many people in other countries believe simply and earnestly that their decisions are not going to affect the spread of nuclear weapons: for them, the sense of energy vulnerability is acute; doom-crying about the coming crisis in the supply of oil intensifies these anxieties. At the same time, domestic nuclear markets in the industrial countries are growing slowly and exports of nuclear technology have become increasingly important in sustaining the technical base, even though the potential export market is small and competition for it is fierce. Furthermore, additional countries have the ambition and means to create major nuclear industries, and the inclination to resist outside restraints; India is a long-standing example, and Brazil is an important recent one. And some governments may simply want to make bombs or at least to shorten the lead time to acquiring them.

Some of these objections are likely to reflect transiently held views; others are likely to be more long-lasting. The sense in Europe and Japan that their nuclear choices make little difference to what happens in the rest of the world, and that what happens elsewhere has little effect on the security of Europe and Japan, could change. The limitations of the technocratic view, which adopts inappropriate criteria such as uranium conservation or breeding ratios as the basis for major national choices instead of focusing on high-level objectives (e.g., least-cost energy, security of supply, properly defined, and the dangers of proliferation) are also becoming slightly clearer over time. For example, a consensus of a sort — that competition for exports should not include offering reprocessing technology as a "sweetener," — is already emerging. A consensus seems likely to emerge also on trade in enrichment technologies and perhaps on trade in breeders.

A key variable here is the degree of commitment to the commercial use of plutonium and to the creation of independent enrichment facilities. Here the record of the last two years since the Ford and Carter initiatives is not encouraging. The British have decided to go ahead with the expansion of the Windscale reprocessing plant, with the purpose of reprocessing spent fuel from Japan, among other countries; the French are going ahead with the expansion of the La Hague reprocessing plant, with similiar intent; and the Japanese have begun to operate their Tokai Mura reprocessing plant. These moves have put the U.S. government in an extremely awkward position: it must approve the transfer of spent fuel for reprocessing. The United States now recognizes that giving approval will help to bring about trade in explosive materials, which is one of the perils we want most to avoid; denying such permission puts us in the position of opposing close allies on an issue to which they have made commitments. It is not difficult to predict that when faced with this dilemma a U.S. president will make the choice that preserves good relations with allies. Indeed, the choices are already being made: approval is being granted on a case-by-case basis for transfers of Japanese spent fuel for reprocessing abroad.

This course opens up the other side of the dilemma. And it transfers much of the burden of responsibility from the United States to France and Britain, as well as to other countries, such as Japan, that seem to be making their nuclear choices largely on the basis of domestic considerations. Should they choose, France and Britain can undoubtedly become plutonium suppliers to the world, or to selected parts of it. But will their politics permit this to happen? Looking ahead to the 1980s, one cannot be confident of either outcome. After all, the major changes in U.S. policy announced by the Ford administration did not originate from the top down; they came about largely as the result of pressure from inside the administration, from Congress, from the Nuclear Regulatory Commission, and from outside groups. In many nations today, attitudes toward nuclear power are polarized, with most of the opposition taking the form of wholesale condemnation; however, the distinction between making nuclear power safer and banning it altogether is likely to emerge more clearly in the future, abroad as well as in the United States. Nor is the behavior of the United States government entirely predictable even when it is not acting under such pressures. (This, of course, is an expressed concern of those dependent on U.S. nuclear-fuel undertakings.) If it should become apparent that the United States, through laxness, is a party to what might increasingly seem to be the nuclear arming of countries, even a president's justifiable concern for his alliance relations might not convince Congress that he has his priorities right.

At this stage one cannot be optimistic that a new and less dangerous set of rules will be adopted. It would be an exaggeration to hold that if these projects go ahead the world will be past the point of no return, but once the British and French governments have invested billions of dollars in expanding capacity at Windscale and La Hague in order to reprocess spent fuel for foreign customers, even with Japan sharing much of the financial burden, it will be politically much more difficult for them to refrain from carrying on with these large-scale export operations.

There are additional—and overdue—steps that the United States should take. The most important is implementing President Carter's offer of October 1977 to have the United States take back some spent fuel from abroad. It would also help if Canada would join with us in such an effort. To improve the security of fuel supply, the United States has recently eased the schedule on which the electric utilities must deliver uranium to the enrichment plants and has consequently helped to reduce the stress on uranium markets. These moves do not directly affect supply security, but by reducing price pressure on the uranium market they do help to dispel a sense of coming shortage. These unilateral actions can be usefully supplemented by the creation of the International Fuel Bank.

Over time, the industrialized countries may lend support to a system constituted along these lines, but many of the developing countries will continue to see things differently. Because security interests predominate for many of them, arms transfers and alliance ties are especially important. The U.S. mood of withdrawal from commitments abroad undermines the international cooperation component of a nonproliferation strategy. At least we should have no illusion about the inconsistency between the objectives of reduced involvement and nonproliferation.

The often implicit, sometimes explicit, assumption in the position taken by Europeans or Japanese, that the phenomenon of proliferation is chiefly a problem for the United States, is by no means self-evident. One might find it easier to make the opposite case. Suppose that these nonproliferation efforts fail. The world is likely to witness not a rush to get explosives, but rather an edging toward a capacity to make them, especially on the part of developing countries outside the principal alliance systems—primarily those who fear their more powerful rivals or are uncertain about possible development of nuclear bombs by regional rivals. These uncertainties and reciprocal fears could well drive many countries to the brink. Some would probably go over. Under these circumstances, the United States, because it can withdraw behind its ocean barriers, would be less subject to pressures than would Europe or Japan.

Such a state of nuclear tension would not be promising for the continued development of civilian nuclear power. Current popular opposition would seem tame by comparison with what could develop. In a world in which many countries were on the point of deploying nuclear weapons, we would be devising very different strategies. Perspectives have changed a great deal in recent years, and more changes are in store during INFCE and beyond. The certainty of change is the linchpin of the argument that irrevocable commitments should be avoided.

Notes

1. These points were made by Victor Gilinsky of the U.S. Nuclear Regulatory Commission in remarks to the Atomic Industrial Forum/British Nuclear Forum International Conference on the Nuclear Fuel Cycle, London, September 28, 1978.

18
Comments on Mr. Rowen's Position

Ryukichi Imai

Strangely enough, what concerns me most about Rowen's text is its excellence. He has written a very well organized exposé of basic U.S. viewpoints, concerns, and proposals regarding nuclear nonproliferation. It should be well received within the United States, and that is exactly what makes me uneasy: his analysis will not enjoy universal acceptance outside the United States. Apart from the problem of determining whose view is closer to the truth—assuming there is such a thing as truth on the subject of nonproliferation—it seems to me important to recognize that the very fact of deep disagreement does damage to the worldwide cause of nuclear nonproliferation, which we all recognize to be one of the most crucial issues of our time. The basic intention of my own contribution was to point this out and to urge that disagreement not be allowed to develop into the basis for serious (and unnecessary) discord within the industrialized world. I am concerned to deal here chiefly with this somewhat general problem, rather than to take up Rowen's arguments point by point. Inevitably, I shall repeat some of the main points of my own text.

Addressed individually, and independently of the larger framework of the issue, most of Rowen's points are valid and useful. Some of his remarks, at least, are to me matters of opinion about which everyone is entitled to his view, whether or not my own happens to differ from his. But "matters of opinion" can become crucial problems depending on how they are espoused in national policies in the real world. What worries Western Europe and Japan about the current U.S. nonproliferation policy is its intent to alter unilaterally the accepted norm of the nuclear world, which, after all, had been the norm so vigorously promoted by that same United States up to just a few years ago. Rowen, to be sure, was not among the promoters of a plutonium economy, but the abrupt manner in which U.S. nuclear policy shifted from the stand taken by his opponents to the position he advocates was very disquieting.

In the view of many, nuclear matters do not exist as an abstract problem, but rather are intimately related to many other aspects of international relations that, taken together, determine different countries' varying perceptions of military or economic security. The passage of domestic law that appears to ignore that reality—and declares in essence that the United States will employ its position as supplier of enrichment services to the world as leverage in enforcing the 1978 version of truth U.S. style—is taken abroad as a very illuminating sign of the direction that U.S. foreign policy in general may be taking.

I shall direct my response, then, chiefly to underlying philosophy and some specific principles—and give least attention to details. The opening paragraph of my own text made three points.

1. Nonproliferation has been primarily a U.S. concern with which other countries have gone along.

2. Nonproliferation has too often been treated as a technological and procedural matter, and its being treated as such has tended to impede popular understanding of the issue.

3. The credibility of specific nonproliferation proposals advanced by the United States has unfortunately been rather low, partly because of the frequency with which U.S. policies have shifted.

Seen in the light of the 1978 proposals, these points immediately foster two further, crucially important, observations:

4. It has been undoubtedly very useful and necessary that, at this juncture in the history of nuclear power, the United States took vigorous steps to remind the world of the critical significance of this issue.

5. Given the power of U.S. influence over matters of nuclear energy, it is extremely important that the United States weigh the validity of other points of view and formulate their policies on a realistic and credible basis.

My own text was an attempt to present Japanese views of the

"realistic" and the "credible" without denying the validity of the major U.S. concerns. Furthermore, I have attempted to define more clearly — more realistically — the basic nonproliferation concern of our time. It is one thing to ponder the subject as a universal, long-term issue; in that light, the great nuclear arsenals of the superpowers and their continuing escalation cannot escape scrutiny. But it is quite another thing to search for a nonproliferation system that might reduce the more specific and better identified risks. That approach, in fact, accords well with the U.S. posture regarding its own strategic and tactical nuclear weapons. By contrast, the inadvertent mixing of idealism and realism in problem-solving can create a situation in which friends are poorly served while adversaries benefit from the confusion within the alliance. It is a matter of deep concern that after a quarter-century of amicable U.S.-Japan relations, the problem of energy and its economics might breed genuine discord between the two countries. I have personally witnessed, during the 1977 Tokai Mura reprocessing negotiations, how insensitivities to each other's basic needs and political realities can easily lead to unnecessary confrontations of national policies and sentiments.

The first issue that comes to mind under the rubric of underlying philosophy is what might be described as a "lack of a sense of history," and it is such a lack that I detect in the basic U.S. approach. Rather, one is impressed by the seeming U.S. interest in "taking charge of human destiny." Put another way, the U.S. attitude represents "a basic unwillingness to accept uncertainty as an ingredient of the future world," but instead tries to write its own (and others') policies on the basis of precise systems analyses of the future. This approach leads to black-and-white rejection of one scenario in favor of another. In the traditional Japanese view, man can seldom overcome the uncertainties of his circumstances, and we may be living in a time in which man must learn to live with a range of unparalleled uncertainties in both knowledge and forecasts — in which he must base policy on an array of options of shifting viability. This is the case not only with nuclear matters, but with energy in general, as well as with a whole spectrum of other subjects bearing on national security. The problem here is not to ask which approach is right. The difference in approaches is due partly to differences in cultural traditions, partly to different perceptions of man's ability to influence the course of history.

In assessing postwar history, it is clear that we have come to a time of major change in the values that have dominated the past quarter-century. The credibility of Big Science and Big Technology seems to be eroding throughout the world. Besides the relentlessly escalating nuclear competition between East and West, there is an emerging confrontation between North and South, as symbolized by calls for a new international economic order. Instead of maintaining a high-growth economy, in which demand always creates supply, the world is plunging into a period in which supply restrains demand. All of these shifts are related to the basic structure of the world order and thus have an important influence on the problem of nuclear nonproliferation. When one confronts a global issue that will affect the fate of mankind in the coming ten or twenty years, it becomes clear that a sense of history will play an essential role. Given the complexity of the world today, the ability of man to engineer history is necessarily limited. Those who are undeterred in their faith that man can do so are driven by what is often called a sense of "missionary purpose." Again, I do not want to be seen as denying the role of missionary purpose in history. In fact, any analysis of a proposal must combine elements of optimistic idealism and pessimistic realism. The U.S. approach, characterized by Rowen's text, tends to be overly pessimistic about the inevitability of U.S.-Soviet nuclear confrontation and excessively optimistic about the possibilities for an international nonproliferation regime based on worldwide consensus on alternative fuel cycles, the viability of CIVEX technology, and an international guarantee of fuel supply. Each of these issues harbors treacherous industrial, technical, legal, economic, or political problems.

The mix of idealism and realism of course varies from country to country, depending on such conditions as access to raw materials, degree of regional and national political and military stability, and internal strengths and weaknesses. It would be difficult, and probably inappropriate, to pass judgment respecting which country's mix most closely approximates rationality, since the different approaches reflect mainly differences in the conditions faced. The variation in approach may also reflect differences in the way countries perceive the fundamental nature of modern industrial technology, as well as differences in their confidence to assess and forecast the impact of technological development. Each of these subjects is complex and requires extensive, sophisticated study. The public discussion of nonproliferaton leads inevitably to a simplification of these issues in ways that mislead the public and impede real understanding.

Moreover, there is a tendency to mix important long-term issues with the particularities of a point in time. Some specifics will serve to illustrate this point. For example, long-term trends in nuclear economics are often analyzed on the basis of detailed breakdowns of power costs — estimates of uranium-ore prices, enrichment costs, construction and operating costs of power plants, reprocessing costs, and the monetary value of the plutonium thus extracted. Figures for the future represent best estimates based on present knowledge, and they may be no more accurate than the figures given ten years ago. This is particularly true when one is talking about anticipated costs twenty years hence. Ten years ago, predictions of mils per kilowatt-hour of nuclear power generation in 1985 were much more optimistic than they are today. Added safety and environmental constraints, as well as the increasing difficulty of assessing fuel-cycle costs, have made the costs of power stations — nuclear, coal-fired, or oil-fired — higher and less predictable. All forms of energy have become more costly, more uncertain, and the utility of cost comparisons, as a tool of policy formulation, is declining. If cost is the dominant consideration, why are we even talking about nuclear fusion or solar energy?

It is a mistake to take illustrative examples as if they were established truths. As a basis for national policy, contingency considerations are always more important than specific figures. Numbers must, of course, be used to guide policy judgments, but devising contingency plans is more to the point, for the figures may turn out to be wrong. In this connection, it is worth noting that some countries are endowed with brighter prospects than others and accordingly can pursue current policies with greater confidence. They also have much greater latitude to alter their policies later, should that become necessary. Others simply cannot do that — cannot base national survival squarely on the judgments of the moment.

Rowen appreciates the delicacy of establishing a line between those who are qualified to develop plutonium technology and those who are not. The choice is between adhering to a principle of universality, which would lead to the estrangement of important U.S. allies in the industrialized world, and establishing an exclusivity that fits the realities of geopolitics and technology and has therefore a chance to achieve the basic objectives of nonproliferation. The latter course is admittedly difficult, especially in view of the growing North-South confrontation. It can lead to the alienation of some Third World countries. But an effort to invent reasons why the *industrialized* nations should not feel estranged by a policy of universality will not change the reality. To avoid drawing the line between qualified and unqualified just because the task is difficult raises questions about the seriousness of the commitment to resolve the proliferation problem. Since a major campaign to establish the lines has already begun, one might as well face up to the fundamental issue. Rowen agrees that the central issue is not the acquisition of nuclear armament by the industrialized nations, but rather the proliferation of nuclear weapons capabilities in the Third World; he agrees that those who should be most seriously concerned about the latter prospect are the countries of the North. It seems to me obvious, then, that it falls to the North to devise means of preventing the transfer of dangerous nuclear technologies to the South, no matter how difficult that may be. If the task turns out to be impossible, then there is no way to stop nuclear proliferation.

One can argue that the whole issue of nuclear proliferation is related to discrimination among sovereign states and thus raises basic issues of national sovereignty. To assume that the essential characteristics of nation-states may be ignored in the implementation of nonproliferation measures is utopian. Faced with external pressures to impose restraints based on some universal good, the sovereign nation has the prerogative, at least in theory, to determine priorities reflecting its own perception of threats to its national security. It makes more sense, then—and is more credible—to treat the entire nonproliferation issue from the point of view of U.S. national interests and to seek grounds on which those interests might be found to be compatible with the similar self-interests of as many of the other influential countries as possible. That approach, which is in fact customary with respect to most problems, accommodates the pursuit of worldwide nonproliferation without necessarily denying the role of fast breeder reactors, whether on technical or economic grounds.

The abundance of uranium is one of the central themes of the latest U.S. nonproliferation proposal. Its basic logic seems to run as follows: because there is sufficient uranium to drive light-water reactors for some time to come, there will probably be no need for plutonium before the next major energy technology emerges. There are three problems with this contention. First, one can never be certain about the extent of reserves of mineral resources. To be sure, there is uranium in great abundance, if one contemplates only the 4 billion tons believed to lie beneath the oceans. But the problem has always been the question of what is economical; reserves become meaningful only when they are marketable, and judgments of marketability always rest with the owner of the reserves or those in a position to invest. Whoever is in such a position is guided by his view of future market conditions, as well as by the availability of funds on a cash-flow basis. For a mineral like uranium, which reaches the market roughly ten years after preparations for its extraction have begun, and which can be used only for the generation of nuclear power, this judgment is difficult in the extreme. Second, reserve figures are those of the individual mining operations, which are chronically prone to manipulate reserve figures in the name of maximizing profit expectations. The third problem concerns the time during which uranium is expected to last. Many claim that by the year 2020 fusion or solar energy or "something else" will be able to take over. There is certainly no technical justification for such an assumption. It is indeed stunning that he who can be so overly pessimistic about plutonium-fueled fast breeder reactors as industrial energy producers can at the same time be so optimistic about the prospects for other technologies, the little-known and even the unknown. The history of modern technology indicates that it will take fifty to sixty years for any major energy technology to penetrate the market sufficiently to supply a major portion of total energy demand. This is due to social inertia and to limitations on the rate of industrial growth. As a future option, the fast breeder reactor is far more realistic than either fusion or solar energy.

The maximum size for a complete light-water reactor industry—i.e., reactor supply, fuel cycle, management of research and development, operator training, etc.—is said to be about 50 GW_e, or about fifty power stations operating at the 1 GW_e level. Since the technology of fast breeder reactors is more complex, based as it is on an extension of the light-water reactor, it is safe to assume that its development will require an even larger minimum industrial base. This leads to two conclusions. First, none of the Third World countries seems likely to develop industries on such a scale; thus, insofar as industrial logic is concerned, there is no justifiable basis for the development of plutonium works in any Third World country. If national prestige were not a factor, and the usual logic of industrial technology were permitted to run its course, Third World nuclear proliferation would not be a serious risk. This is true with respect not only to plutonium, but also to enrichment and other forms of nuclear research and development. The Third World is dotted with abandoned research reactors provided during the early phase of the U.S. Atoms for Peace program, in many cases acquired simply in the name of national prestige.

Second, in order to assure long-term fuel supply as a universal proposal, one must supply fuel to the entire 50 GW_e light-water reactor complex, and the experience of the world in nuclear and other commodity transfers provides convincing proof that this, too, is unrealistic. Even excepting the 1973 oil crisis, there is ample evidence that international trade in energy resources is no longer governed by the time-honored market mechanism. This point is borne out very clearly by the restrictive policies on uranium export recently adopted by Australia and Canada, and the U.S. Nonproliferation Act of 1978 offers further evidence. Supply guarantees are feasible only when they relate to small amounts and short periods—for example, guarantees made to Third World countries in return for their subscription to particular nonproliferation agreements. One should add that the use of plutonium as a near-term fuel for light-water reactors should be viewed with skepticism, since it offers, to anyone who owns a single light-water reactor plant, a pretext to handle plutonium.

The weaknesses within the NPT system are no new discovery. There are problems with the establishment and maintenance of safeguards. Indeed, there are logical inconsistencies within Article III. And as has often been noted, the more basic weaknesses in logic lie in Articles I and II—namely, in the provisions that give special status to the five nuclear weapons states. Why is five a special number? Why would a world with five such states be safer than one with four or six? All of these weaknesses have been absorbed into the text of the NPT — as compromises that were needed in order to produce a treaty, which all agreed would be a valuable first step toward nuclear stability and nonproliferation. The NPT represents political realism rather than logic, and as such is expected to contain weaknesses. It is in this sense that the world community will resist any move that would break the basic trust of the NPT. If there is a need for further modification of the provisions of the NPT in order to better address the world situation of the 1980s, the proper starting point is not the public degrading of NPT credibility and effectiveness.

Much of the detail in my own text constitutes comment on Rowen's many points. My purpose here, as noted at the outset, has been simply to expose readers to a certain lack of accord between U.S. nonproliferation policy and the views of the rest of the world. Unless something is done, these differences could take on dangerous proportions. To summarize, nonproliferation seems to me a problem of clarifying political relations among nation-states, not of technical or economic evaluation of the future role of fast breeder reactors.

Appendixes

Appendix

Appendix A:
United States–Japan
Tokai Mura Agreement
Joint Communiqué
September 12, 1977

I

Negotiations between the Governments of Japan and the United States of America concerning the operation, in accordance with the Agreement of Cooperation between the Government of Japan and the Government of the United States of America Concerning Civil Uses of Atomic Energy of February 26, 1968, as amended (hereinafter referred to as "the Agreement for Cooperation"), of the Tokai Reprocessing Facility (hereinafter referred to as "the Facility") were held in Tokyo from August 29 to September 1, 1977. The Japanese delegation was led by H. E. Mr. Sosuko Uno, Minister of State for Science and Technology and Chairman of the Atomic Energy Commission, while the United States delegation was headed by H. E. Ambassador Gerard Smith, Special Representative for Non-Proliferation Matters. The negotiations were conducted in a frank and friendly atmosphere throughout the session.

II

·The United States recognizes the importance of the development of nuclear energy for the energy security and economic development of Japan. The United States strongly supports continued development of peaceful uses of nuclear energy in Japan. The United States is prepared to cooperate with Japan for the purpose of assuring that Japan's long-term nuclear energy programs, including its breeder research and development program, not be prejudiced. The United States is prepared to work with Japan and other countries to establish arrangements for assured supply of natural and low enriched uranium. The United States affirms that its policy is to accord Japan non-discriminatory treatment in the field of the peaceful uses of nuclear energy.

Japan and the United States will cooperate in evaluating the nuclear fuel cycle and the future role of plutonium. They share the view that plutonium poses a serious proliferation danger, that its recycling in light water reactors is not ready at present for commercial use, and that its premature commercialization should be avoided. They equally share the view that, if separation of plutonium for research and development work on fast breeder reactors and other advanced reactors is carried out, it should be at a rate not exceeding actual plutonium needs for such purposes.

Both Japan and the United States intend to defer decisions relating to the commercial use of plutonium in light water reactors at least during the International Nuclear Fuel Cycle Evaluation Program (INFCEP), which is expected to continue for two yars. Japan plans to do related research and development work involving several kilograms of plutonium during this period. Furthermore, Japan and the United States do not intend to undertake any major moves regarding additional reprocessing facilities for plutonium separation during the above-mentioned period. Thereafter, when making decisions on such facilities, they intend to take into account the outcome of the INFCEP, including spent fuel storage possibilities and other technical and institutional alternatives to reprocessing.

III

Taking into account both immediate practical considerations and the desire of the parties to identify fuel cycles that are as proliferation resistant as possible, the parties reached an understanding that the operation of the Facility will be guided, for an initial period of two years, by the following principles, in accordance with the relevant laws and regulations of Japan:

1. The Facility will process up to 99 tonnes of U.S.-origin spent fuel. The major portion of this spent fuel will be processed in the scheduled mode to prove out plant design and to preserve Japan's warranty rights. Some of this spent fuel may be used for the experimental coprocessing described in paragraph 4 below.

2. Japan intends to defer, during the initial period of operation, the construction of the plutonium conversion facility scheduled to be attached to the Facility.

3. The United States is prepared to consider with Japan on an annual basis Japanese plutonium requirements for advanced reactor research and development and to seek ways to ensure that any shortfalls of plutonium resulting from deferral of the construction of the plutonium conversion facility referred to in the preceding paragraph will not entail unnecessary

delay in the Japanese program.

4. Experimental coprocessing will be undertaken in the Operational Test Laboratory (OTL) at the Facility and in other facilities, during the period when the main Facility is operating in the scheduled mode. The results of this experimental work will be made available to INFCEP in support of the INFCEP effort to identify fuel cycles that are as proliferation resistant as the "once through" fuel cycle.

5. At the end of the initial period of operation, the mode of operating the Facility will be promptly converted from conventional reprocessing to full-scale coprocessing, if such coprocessing is agreed by the two Governments to be technically feasible and effective as a result of the experimental work in the OTL and in the light of the results of INFCEP. The necessary modifications of the Facility will be carried out in such a way as to assure that the expenditures and delays involved are kept to the minimum consistent with fulfilling the purposes of these principles, and that the operation of the Facility may start expeditiously in the coprocessing mode.

6. The International Atomic Energy Agency (IAEA) will be afforded full opportunity to apply safeguards at the Facility, including continuous inspection, in accordance with the relevant existing and future international agreements. Japan is willing to improve the safeguardability and physical security at the Facility, and for this purpose is prepared to cooperate with the IAEA in the testing of advanced safeguards instrumentation, and to make timely preparations to facilitate the use of such instrumentation in the initial period. The United States is prepared to participate in this safeguards testing through agreed means. Japan and the United States will promptly consult with the IAEA to facilitate implementation of this testing program. The results of this safeguards experimentation will be made available to INFCEP.

IV

On the basis of the understandings, principles and intentions set out above, and in view of Japan's continued adherence to the Non-Proliferation Treaty and its undertakings herein with respect to safeguards, the limited amount of plutonium involved, the carefully monitored experimental character of the process, and the provisions for the application of effective safeguards by the IAEA and for advanced safeguards experimentation, a joint determination has been made pursuant to Article VIII C of the Agreement for Cooperation that the provisions of Article XI of that Agreement may be effectively applied to the reprocessing at the Facility of irradiated fuel elements containing up to 99 tonnes of fuel material received from the United States.

Japan and the United States will consult on a regular basis, or at the request of either of the parties, on the implementation of the above-mentioned matters and on any matters related to the Agreement for Cooperation between the two countries.

Appendix B:
Joint Determination for Reprocessing of Special Nuclear Material of United States Origin

On the basis of the understandings, principles and intentions set out in the Communiqué of the Government of Japan and the Government of the United States of America issued on September 12, 1977, and in view of Japan's continued adherence to the Treaty on the Non-Proliferation of Nuclear Weapons and its undertakings therein with respect to safeguards, the limited amount of plutonium involved, the carefully monitored experimental character of the process, and the provisions for the application of effective safeguards by the International Atomic Energy Agency and for advanced safeguards experimentation,

1. The Government of Japan and the Government of the United States of America hereby jointly determine pursuant to Article VIII C of the Agreement for Cooperation between the Government of Japan and the Government of the United States of America Concerning Civil Uses of Atomic Energy of February 26, 1968, as amended, that the provisions of Article XI of that Agreement may be effectively applied to the reprocessing in the Tokai Facility of the Power Reactor and Nuclear Fuel Development Corporation of irradiated fuel elements containing up to 99 tonnes of fuel material received from the United States;

2. No determination is now being made as to whether safeguards can be effectively applied to Purex reprocessing plants in general;

3. There is no change in the requirement for subsequent determinations as to whether the provisions of Article XI may be effectively applied to the reprocessing or other alteration in form or content of any special nuclear material or irradiated fuel elements subject to Article VIII C beyond the irradiated fuel elements referred to in paragraph 1 above. However, the United States would be prepared to enter into an affirmative joint determination, if the mode of operating the said facility is

converted to full-scale coprocessing, subject to the requirements of its laws and mutual agreement on the scope and character of the coprocessing operation.

September 12, 1977

For the Government of Japan:

For the Government of the
United States of America:

Appendix C:
Final Communiqué of the Organizing Conference of the International Nuclear Fuel-Cycle Evaluation, October 21, 1977

The participants in the Organizing Conference of the International Nuclear Fuel Cycle Evaluation are conscious of the urgent need to meet the world's energy requirements and that nuclear energy for peaceful purposes should be made widely available to that end. They are also convinced that effective measures can and should be taken at the national level and through international agreements to minimize the danger of the proliferation of nuclear weapons without jeopardizing energy supplies or the development of nuclear energy for peaceful purposes.

The following countries which participated in the Organizing Conference have therefore agreed that an International Nuclear Fuel Cycle Evaluation (INFCE) will be conducted to explore the best means of advancing these objectives:

Algeria	Japan
Argentina	Korea
Australia	Mexico
Austria	Netherlands
Belgium	Nigeria
Brazil	Norway
Canada	Pakistan
Czechoslovakia	Philippines
Denmark	Poland
Egypt	Portugal
Finland	Romania
France	Spain
German Democratic Republic	Sweden
Federal Republic of Germany	Switzerland
India	Turkey
Indonesia	USSR
Iran	United Kingdom
Ireland	United States
Israel	Venezuela
Italy	Yugoslavia

The Organizing Conference was also attended by representatives of the International Atomic Energy Agency, the Commission of the European Communities, the International Energy Agency, and the Nuclear Energy Agency, who expresssed their willingness to participate in INFCE.

The participants agreed that all interested states and relevant international bodies may participate in the future work of INFCE. It was also agreed that all participants will have an equal opportunity to contribute to that work.

They are aware of the vital importance of preventing proliferation and, moreover, of effective and urgent measures to stop and reverse the nuclear arms race among the nuclear weapons states.

The evaluation will be conducted along lines set out in the attached document entitled "International Nuclear Fuel Cycle Evaluation: Technical and Economic Scope and Methods of Work." The participants recognized that special consideration should also be given to the specific needs of and conditions in developing countries.

The participants agreed that INFCE was to be a technical and analytical study and not a negotiation. The results will be transmitted to governments for their consideration in developing their nuclear energy policies and in international discussions concerning nuclear energy cooperation and related controls and safeguards. Participants would not be committed to INFCE's results.

The evaluation will be carried out in a spirit of objectivity, with mutual respect for each country's choices and decisions in this field, without jeopardizing their respective fuel cycle policies or international cooperation, agreements, and contracts for the peaceful use of nuclear energy, provided that agreed safeguards measures are applied.

The participants welcomed the decision, in principle, of the International Atomic Energy Agency to support INFCE by providing appropriate technical and secretariat assistance. They expressed the hope that the extent and scope of such support will be considered by the appropriate bodies of IAEA. At the same time, they also expressed their hope that the IAEA will play an active role in the conduct of INFCE at all levels and particularly in the area of technical coordination. The participants acknowledge in this connection the dual responsibility of the IAEA in promoting and safeguarding nuclear activities.

The texts of the documents comprising the substantive work of the Evaluation will be made available to all governments and international bodies which express an interest in them.

INTERNATIONAL NUCLEAR FUEL-CYCLE EVALUATION:
TECHNICAL AND ECONOMIC SCOPE AND METHODS OF WORK

I. Technical and Economic Scope
  A. Fuel and Heavy Water Availability
    1. Estimated needs for nuclear energy, and correlated needs for uranium and heavy water, according to different fuel cycle strategies
    2. Uranium availability
       a. assessment of resources and production capacities
       b. policies and incentives for encouraging exploration and production including joint ventures
       c. marketing policies and/or guarantees of sales for companies investing in exploration and production
       d. marketing policies and/or guarantees of supply for utilities
       e. technical development of exploration, mining, and milling methods
    3. Heavy water availability
    4. Thorium availability
    5. Special needs of developing countries
  B. Enrichment Availability
    1. Enrichment needs and availability according to various fuel cycle strategies
       a. joint planning of future capacities
       b. opportunities for cross-investment
       c. freedom of choice for customers in an open market
    2. Technical and economic assessment of the different enrichment technologies
    3. Assessment and comparison of the proliferation risks of the various enrichment techniques
    4. Safeguards aspects specific to enrichment
    5. Multinational or regional fuel cycle centers or similar arrangements
    6. Special needs of developing countries
  C. Assurances of Long-Term Supply of Technology, Fuel and Heavy Water and Services in the Interest of National Needs Consistent with Non-Proliferation
    1. Incentives for long-term commercial contracts between suppliers and consumers, including factors affecting market

stability, e.g., supply, demand and prices
2. Guarantees of assured supply in the context of national import, export and non-proliferation policies
3. Multinational or international mechanisms guaranteeing timely deliveries in case of delays or cut-off of supplies
4. Possible exchange or credit of plutonium for other nuclear fuels
5. Special needs of developing countries

D. Reprocessing, Plutonium Handling, Recycle
1. Reprocessing
   a. study of the technological, economic, environmental and energy aspects of reprocessing on a full industrial scale
   b. safeguards aspects specific to reprocessing
   c. multinational or regional fuel cycle centers or similar arrangements
   d. alernative reprocessing methods
   e. influence of reprocessing schemes on waste conditioning and disposal strategies and economics
2. Plutonium handling
   a. possible conditions and restrictions for adequate storage, transport and use of highly concentrated plutonium
   b. international control of separated plutonium (including storage under the auspices of the IAEA and related availability criteria)
   c. alternative handling methods including spiking or delivery of plutonium in the form of mixed oxide or fuel elements, possibly pre-irradiated
3. Recycle in thermal reactors
   a. study of the technological, economic, environmental and energy aspects of the concept on an industrial scale
   b. safeguards aspects specific to recycling
   c. possible uranium-only recycle
4. Special needs of developing countries

E. Fast Breeders
1. Study of the technological, economic, environmental and energy aspects of the concept on an industrial scale
2. Safeguards aspects specific to fast breeders
3. Reprocessing modes, including:
   a. study of the technological, economic, environmental and energy aspects of reprocessing on a full industrial scale

   b. safeguards aspects specific to fast breeder reprocessing
   c. multinational or regional fuel cycle centers or similar arrangements
   d. alternate reprocessing methods
   4. Special needs of the developing countries
F.   Spent Fuel Management
   1. Storage strategies and costs
      a. for light-water reactors
      b. for heavy-water reactors
      c. for gas-cooled reactors
      d. for fast breeder reactors
   2. Short-term/intermediate storage
      a. assessment of current storage capabilities
      b. ways of increasing spent fuel storage
      c. siting and transportation problems
      d. more efficient utilization of existing spent fuel capacity
      e. institutional, environmental, safeguards, and safety aspects including fuel integrity problems and associated risks
      f. costs
      g. legal matters
   3. Special needs of the developing countries
G.   Waste Management and Disposal
   1. Technology for handling and disposal
      a. spent fuel
      b. separated waste products
   2. Repositories (permanent or retrievable)
      a. siting problems
      b. possibilities or risks of further recovery
      c. institutional, environmental and safety aspects including repository integrity problems and geologic risks and protection against possible dissemination of fission products
      d. costs
      e. legal matters
   3. Special needs of the developing countries
H.   Advanced Fuel Cycle and Reactor Concepts
   1. Once-through fuel utilization for present thermal reactors
      a. methods to increase once-through fuel utilization
      b. optimized fuel and loading designs
      c. tandem cycle
      d. spectral shift

    e. energy balance and economic safeguarding and environmental aspects of once-through utilization

    f. for light-water reactors

    g. for heavy-water reactors

    h. gas-cooled reactors

2. Other reactors and fuel cycle concepts

    a. production utilization and safeguards of high-enriched uranium for power reactors

    b. research reactors: (use of highly-enriched uranium and possible alternatives)

    c. thorium-U-233 cycle

    d. light-water and thorium breeder concepts

    e. high temperature reactors

    f. additional advanced reactor concepts including fusion and spallation breeder reactors with, when relevant, in each case

      • identification of the fuel cycle stages at which nuclear weapons usable material may be separated, and the possible means of minimizing proliferation risks

      • economic, environmental and energy aspects

      • commercialization lead-times

      • safety problems

3. Special needs of developing countries

II. Organization

  A. One international working group is created for each of the aforementioned chapters, composed of all states desiring to make a contribution to their work. Designated co-chairmen of these eight working groups are as follows:

Group 1:	Co-Chairmen—Canada, Egypt, India
Group 2:	Co-Chairmen—France, Federal Republic of Germany, Iran
Group 3:	Co-Chairmen—Australia, Philippines, Switzerland
Group 4:	Co-Chairmen—Japan, United Kingdom
Group 5:	Co-Chairmen—Belgium, Italy, USSR
Group 6:	Co-Chairmen—Argentina, Spain
Group 7:	Co-Chairmen—Finland, Netherlands, Sweden
Group 8:	Co-Chairmen—Republic of Korea, Romania, USA

  B. Each group will decide, after consultation as appropriate with the chairmen of other related groups, whether or not subgroups, which would report to the group, should be created. There would not be common funding of the studies, each participating country, including those providing chairmen, being responsible for the expenses of its own participation. Each group or sub-group would distribute its work among its members. Cooperative studies among national organizations or industries of participating countries would be organized to the extent possible. Contribution by a participating country would be welcome.

C. In order to enable the various groups to gather complete and realistic information in their respective fields, all participants will facilitate the exchange of the data necessary for the completion of the evaluation program.

D. The various groups will report to a plenary conference of the participants which will meet at least once a year. The next plenary conference should convene in Vienna in approximately one year. The studies should be completed in two years or less. These reports and these studies will be primarily technical and analytical. Where agreed positions are reached, a consensus will be expressed, but each participant would be entitled to a dissenting or separate opinion if it so wished, which would be included in the report of the working group. The final plenary conference of the participating countries will be held approximately two years from now.

E. A Technical Coordinating Committee composed of the co-chairmen of the working groups will be convened every six months, or as otherwise agreed, to coordinate the work of the various groups from the technical point of view. Other participating parties may attend as observers. The first meeting of the Technical Coordinating Committee will be held in Vienna beginning December 12, 1977 at the facilities of the IAEA. The Technical Coordinating Committee will report to the Plenary Conference.

F. The work of the evaluation will make use of the capabilities of the IAEA. The IAEA may be represented in all groups and sub-groups participating in the program, and in the Technical Coordinating Committee. The agency may be asked, in particular, to provide secretariat services. Other relevant international and intergovernmental bodies are invited to participate in the working groups.

Appendix D:
Brief Summary of the "Nuclear Non-Proliferation Act of 1978"

The Nuclear Non-Proliferation Act of 1978 is the most comprehensive public law dealing with nuclear exports legislated since the passage of the Atomic Energy Act of 1954. It contains the conditions and criteria which will govern U.S. cooperation with other nations in the peaceful use of nuclear energy, and seeks to balance concern over the dangers of nuclear proliferation with the legitimate use of peaceful nuclear power to meet energy demands. Central to the Act is encouragement for universal ratification of the Non-Proliferation Treaty, and a comprehensive set of controls, procedures and incentives designed to provide a framework for predictable international nuclear cooperation and commerce, to enhance the reliability of the United States as a nuclear supplier, and to limit the further diffusion of nuclear explosive capabilities.

SUMMARY OF THE ACT

Overview

The Act specifies *controls*; *procedures*; and *incentives*. The principal *controls* include:

1. requiring, in any new or amended agreement, and after twenty-four months from enactment of the law for licenses under existing agreements, IAEA safeguards on all nuclear activities in non-nuclear weapons states as a condition for continued cooperation with the United States;
2. defining immediate export licensing criteria for cooperation under existing agreements, pending renegotiation;
3. establishing additional criteria above and beyond those which ap-

Prepared by the U.S. Department of State.

ply to existing agreements for new and amended agreements for
cooperation;

4. requiring the USG to undertake to renegotiate all existing
    agreements to achieve conformity with the new criteria and condi-
    tions;

5. mandating a cut-off of cooperation if a non-nuclear-weapons state
    detonates a nuclear explosive device after the date of enactment,
    or terminates IAEA safeguards, or materially violates a U.S.
    cooperation agreement.

In addition to setting forth the controls that will apply in agreements
involving U.S. nuclear cooperation, the Act also introduces new *procedures* designed to minimize delays in the U.S. nuclear export process
and to maximize predictability of U.S. export policy. To these ends the
Act includes:

1. a provision for Presidential override of NRC export license denials
    or delays if he judges that it would seriously prejudice U.S. non-
    proliferation objectives or would jeopardize the common defense
    and security not to do so;

2. time limits on Executive Branch consideration and NRC disposi-
    tion of export license applications.

Finally, with a view to facilitating the development of, and access to,
nuclear energy in a way that would support an effective non-proliferation
regime, the Act contains a number of *incentive* measures including:

1. the reevaluation of all aspects of the nuclear fuel cycle jointly with
    other nuclear supplier and recipient states in the International
    Nuclear Fuel-Cycle Evaluation. The objective of this enterprise is
    to identify technological and institutional ways in which to meet
    nuclear energy requirements and related national concerns while
    reinforcing shared non-proliferation goals;

2. efforts to negotiate an International Nuclear Fuel Authority to
    enhance international fuel assurances as well as to meet spent fuel
    and waste disposal concerns, and thereby demonstrate safe and ef-
    fective ways to achieve the objective of efficient and economic
    operation of nuclear power programs consistent with non-
    proliferation;

3. assistance for developing countries in identifying and securing ac-
    cess to non-nuclear energy resources where appropriate and in the
    interest of meeting developing country concerns with social and
    industrial development and reduced external dependence.

Significant Particular Features

While not purporting to be a definitive legal statement of the major features of the Act, for which purpose the legislation itself should be consulted, the following presentation gives a more detailed insight into the Nuclear Non-Proliferation Act.

I. Immediately Applicable Export Licensing Criteria:

In addition to the requirement that an export not be inimical to U.S. common defense and security, specific criteria to be applied to U.S. supply are established for NRC export licensing of nuclear fuel and reactors:

- IAEA safeguards;
- no explosive use;
- maintaining adequate physical security;
- U.S. consent for retransfers;*
- U.S. consent for reprocessing;*
- application of above criteria to materials or equipment produced through any transferred sensitive nuclear technology.

II. Full-Scope Safeguards:

IAEA safeguards on all peaceful nuclear activities in non-nuclear weapons states will be required, after twenty-four months following enactment, as a condition of continued U.S. export. This export licensing criterion may be waived by the President under exceptional circumstances, subject, however, to Congressional veto by concurrent resolution.

III. Criteria for New and Amended Agreements for Cooperation:

Beyond the immediate export criteria, the following additional provisions must be included in new and amended agreements:

- IAEA safeguards of indefinite duration on U.S. supply and, as a continuing condition of U.S. supply on all peaceful nuclear activities in non-nuclear-weapons states;
- return to the U.S. of nuclear materials if a recipient non-

---

*Exports to groups of nations are exempted from the retransfer and reprocessing requirements for twenty-four months (with possible one-year extensions) if they agree to renegotiate.

nuclear-weapons state detonates a nuclear explosive device, terminates a safeguards agreement, or materially violates the cooperation agreement;

- U.S. consent to the retransfer and/or reprocessing of spent fuel irradiated in U.S.-supplied reactors;
- U.S. approval of facilities for storage of weapons usable material;
- application of all of the above conditions to any nuclear materials produced through the use of transferrred sensitive nuclear technology;
- one or more of these requirements may be waived by the President if U.S. non-proliferation objectives or national security would otherwise by jeopardized. New or amended agreements must lie before Congress for sixty days and then come into effect unless the Congress passes a concurrent resolution disapproving the agreement.

IV. Events Requiring Termination of U.S. Nuclear Supply After the Date of Enactment:

A. Exports to any non-nuclear-weapons state will be terminated if that state:

- detonates a nuclear explosive device;
- terminates or abrogates IAEA safeguards;
- is found by the President to have materially violated IAEA safeguards;
- uses nuclear material in activities of direct significance to the acquisition of explosive devices.

B. Exports will be terminated to any state or group of states that:
- violates its agreement for cooperation or other terms of supply;
- assists a non-nuclear-weapons state in activities of direct significance to the acquisition of nuclear explosives;
- enters into an agreement for transferring reprocessing capabilities except in connection with INFCE or a subsequent international arrangement to which the U.S. subscribes.

V. Subsequent Arrangements (under Existing and New Agreements) for Reprocessing and Handling of Spent Fuel:

    A. U.S. consent for reprocessing or transfer of separated plutonium may only be given if it will not result in a significant increase in the risk of proliferation. In making this evaluation, foremost consideration will be given to whether the reprocessing or retransfer will take place under conditions that ensure timely warning to the U.S. of any diversion well in advance of the time at which a non-nuclear-weapons state could transform the diverted material into a nuclear explosive device. There is an exception for reprocessing at facilities that processed power reactor fuel prior to enactment of this legislation but the U.S. must attempt to ensure the same standard is applied to reprocessing at these facilities as well.

    B. Any proposed return of foreign spent fuel to the U.S. would be subject to review by the Executive Branch and the Congress.

VI. Licensing of Nuclear Components not Specifically Covered in the Legislation:

The NRC is directed to define components which are of special relevance for nuclear explosives. These would be licensed by NRC which would determine whether the export was inimical to the common defense and security and the license would also be subject to the following standards:

- IAEA safeguards;
- no explosive pledge;
- no retransfers without U.S. consent.

VII. Export Licensing Procedures with a View to Expediting the Export Licensing Process:

The Act

- requires the NRC to adopt procedures which will be the exclusive basis for hearings before the Commission;
- permits the NRC to issue licenses for multiple shipments or give expedited treatment to follow-on licenses if no material change in circumstances has occurred;

- allows the President to authorize an export after an NRC negative decision, subject to Congressional review and veto;
- mandates the Executive Branch and the NRC normally to act on licenses within sixty days, and
- limits Government-to-Government transfers (without NRC licenses) to small quantities or to emergency situations in order to achieve uniformity in all transactions.

VIII. Fuel Assurances Initiatives:

A. The Secretary of Energy is directed to proceed with the construction and operation of expanded uranium enrichment capacity;

B. The President is directed to study the need for additional U.S. enrichment capacity for foreign and domestic needs and further to report to Congress on the desirability of inviting foreign participation in new U.S. uranium enrichment facilities;

C. The President is also given a mandate to begin the negotiation of an International Nuclear Fuel Authority to provide fuel services, and international spent-fuel repositories;

D. These and other related fuel assurances are intended to apply to countries that adhere to policies designed to prevent further proliferation, and to bring continued use and development of nuclear energy into harmony with international security through non-proliferation.

Index